Psychotherapy
AND THE
CHRISTIAN MESSAGE

BY ALBERT C. OUTLER

Harper ChapelBooks

HARPER & ROW, PUBLISHERS
NEW YORK

CONTENTS

PREFACE

This little book is an essay in clarification. The problem with which it is concerned is how to relate psychotherapy and Christianity in valid synthesis and productive alliance. Since my own seminary days I have been interested in psychotherapy as an important resource for pastoral work. I wrote my B.D. thesis on this topic and got my first clinical training twenty years ago, when it was something of a pioneering venture. In the two decades since, my observations and experiences in counseling, both as pastor and teacher, have greatly strengthened my confidence in the practical usefulness of psychotherapy for the work of the Christian minister, teacher and counselor. And, in my further explorations into theory and further clinical training, it has become increasingly clear that modern psychotherapy is much more than a significant development in the healing arts. It has also come to present a significant opportunity and challenge to Christian thought—one of the most momentous in our time. There is, on the one hand, an important consensus between the two, especially in the practical aspect of interpersonal relations. But there is also an unresolved conflict in theory, and it is this conflict which has created a long-standing confusion that deserves more careful attention than it has, in fact, received. The problem has been prematurely solved in many ways, ranging from outright rejection from one side or the other to amiable agreements to ignore theory as far as possible and concentrate on "practical matters." Many modern Christians have taken as dim a view of psychotherapy as their great-grandfathers took of what was then "the new biology." And the psychotherapists, for the most part, have adopted a world view, not readily compatible with the Christian perspective, without adequate examination and reflection. Thus, on both sides, many of the prior questions have been settled by assumption. This procedure is not quite good enough, either for the empirical enterprise of psychotherapy or for the theological enterprise of Christianity.

In his ordinary collaboration with physicians and surgeons, the Christian can be *relatively* indifferent to their world views and religious beliefs. But the work of the psychotherapist involves the well-being of the whole person in a way which goes beyond the customary medical treatment—and thus requires a more explicit estimate of "the human condition." Nor can the Christian borrow and use the practical wisdom of psychotherapy without testing its presuppositions about human nature and existence. Christianity and psychotherapy are both wisdoms-about-life and it is by no means clear that they are the same wisdom. The convinced Christian, who is also convinced of the immense significance and value of psychotherapy in modern life, must then explore at least some of the basic issues that lie between them and must clarify for himself the problems and the terms of the alliance between them.

This exploration has, of course, already begun. One gets the impression that not many of the psychotherapists are inclined to take the truth claims of Christianity seriously and that a few Christians are inclined to take the truth claims of psychotherapy too seriously. The most notable example of the kind of analysis and appraisal I believe is required is David E. Roberts, *Psychotherapy and a Christian View of Man*. Two important books from the Roman Catholic standpoint are VanderVeldt and Odenwald, *Psychiatry and Catholicism* and Joseph Nuttin, *Psychoanalysis and Personality*. Here, in this present book, I have tried to extend the discussion and, I hope, to stimulate further ferment among all the people who are interested, or ought to be, in the *rapprochement* of the most important of the modern sciences of man and what I believe is the truest wisdom about the nature and destiny of man.

I should wish to address myself to all counselors and therapists (and all others interested in wisdom about human life), whether their faith be Christian or not, but I do not have an equal hope that all will attend. Psychotherapists are not accustomed to read Christian theologians with real attention. And it may be that many counselors would prefer to take the cash of practical endeavor and let the credit of "nonempirical" inquiry go. But the time ripens for new theoretical developments in this whole area and it is my hope that this book will encourage the further examination of basic issues that cannot longer be evaded or managed by implication. There is only one group to which I am sure I have nothing to say: those who are convinced that psychotherapy and Christian thought have nothing to do with each other, or who suppose that the relation between them is already fixed by their respective dogmas.

In a discussion like this, one is partisan without trying and objective only through a conscious and deliberate effort. One cannot avoid having a standpoint. For myself, I have chosen and confirmed the Christian faith as the primary source of whatever wisdom there may be in these pages. But I have also tried to understand the thought and outlook of the psychotherapists I have studied, in full seriousness and with sincere gratitude. And in putting the respective viewpoints side by side for review, I have not supposed that my interpretations had to be definitive in order to illumine the chief contentions under discussion. An argument like this must have an open end and we must have open hearts to find our way beyond the present impasse.

No one is satisfied with the term "psychotherapy," partly because no one can define it to everyone's satisfaction. It is simply a handier way to refer to the broad area of psychological medicine than either psychiatry or psychoanalysis, since they are narrower foci within the larger field. In the course of my reflection and work, I have tried to examine most of the major developments in psychotherapy, especially as they affect the work of the Christian counselor. The nuclear motifs of modern psychotherapy are still those supplied by Freud; they have influenced subsequent development more than they themselves have been altered by it. But I have also tried to recognize the significance of the deviations from Freud and the controversies about psychological "orthodoxy" (a task for which the historical theologian is not ill-prepared). Most of all, I have been interested in the American school of cultural analysts (Sullivan, Horney, Fromm, *et al.*) who have succeeded in synthesizing the biologistic outlook of Freud with the further advances that have been made in our understanding of society and the person. When, therefore, I speak of psychotherapy, I am deliberately throwing a wide (and loose-meshed) net. My aim is to point toward the general phenomenon of psychological medicine; the required distinctions between the various sects and systems will appear in proper place.

It will be unfortunate if the reader wastes much time or energy belaboring the obvious shortcomings of this book. There are many omissions here—and much of the exposition is too brief and summary. But this is not a survey of psychotherapy nor a summary of Christian doctrine. My single intention has been to define the problems of alliance and conflict between psychotherapeutic thought and the Christian message and to analyze four of the basic issues that lie between them. If I have omitted something which would significantly alter the definition here proposed or the issues examined, it will be of great service to have it duly noted. Similarly, if it can be shown that a more adequate exposition would have affected the main lines of the argument, this too would constitute a most welcome criticism. But, most of all, I hope that the book will serve its main purpose of being taken up into the ongoing inquiry about the claims and promises of human wisdom-about-life, which is a common enterprise of both psychotherapy and Christian thought.

The occasion for trying to cast my ideas in this field together into ordered form came in a series of lectureships to which I have had the honor to be invited in the past two years. In April, 1951, I gave two lectures at Vanderbilt University. In February, 1953, I delivered the Peyton Lectures at my own university, and, in March, was Merrick Lecturer at Ohio Wesleyan University. This past October, I gave four lectures on the Mead-Swing Foundation at Oberlin University and in November, lectured as Visiting Scholar at the University Center, Atlanta, Georgia. To my host and auditors at all these places I tender my hearty thanks: and especially to Dean John K. Benton and Chancellor Harvie Branscomb of Vanderbilt; Dean Merrimon Cuninggim and my colleagues at Southern Methodist University; Professor Roy L. Diem and Professor Loyd Easton of Ohio Wesleyan; Professors Walter Horton and Clyde Holbrook at Oberlin; and Director John O. Eidson of the University Center, and Professor Paul L. Garber of Agnes Scott College.

There are many debts of aid and encouragement which cannot be listed in such a preface as this, and which are certainly not discharged by such a book as this. There have been my students at Duke and Yale and Southern Methodist University whose problems and questions have taught me at least as much as I was ever able to teach them; more than this, there have also been the numerous opportunities for pastoral counseling that have come my way. And, in the project of the book itself, I have had both the encouragement and the expert aid of the staff in the Religious Book Department of Harper & Brothers. Mr. Decherd Turner, of our own Bridwell Library here at Southern Methodist University has rendered invaluable bibliographical service and has also kindly read the proofs. Mrs. Hollis Huston, Mrs. Audrey Hale, Mrs. Juanita Powers and Mrs. Velma Bedwell gave much needed secretarial assistance at different stages of the project. Finally, I wish to record my gratitude to the following "mentors" and friends who have been greatly useful in the shaping of my understanding of the problems here discussed but who share no responsibility whatever in the faults and shortcomings which still remain after all their efforts: Professor Lavens Thomas, II, who first set me to work in the field; my former colleagues, Robert L. Calhoun and Julian N. Hartt of Yale; Professor David E. Roberts of Union Theological Seminary and the Reverend Otis Rice of St. Luke's Hospital, New York City; Drs. Stanley M. Leavy of New Haven and David Chrzanowski and Harry Bone of the staff of the William Alanson White Institute of Psychiatry. My wife, who has done much of the drudgery of the book, also classifies as *magistra,* for she has "taught" our whole family much in the way of the concrete expression of Christian faith and sanity in zestful living. To her the book is dedicated.

ALBERT OUTLER

Southern Methodist University
Thanksgiving, 1953

CHAPTER ONE

Allies and Rivals

Modern psychotherapy has set an unmistakable mark on modern life. It has come to hold a solid and undisputed place among the healing arts and it has widely affected much of current medical theory and practice. It is at once the least "scientific" of all the branches of medicine and the one most fully concerned with the total person. Because of this concern, psychotherapeutic theory has extended far beyond the clinic to develop a comprehensive account of human behavior in its disorder and repair. Its basic ideas about the different levels of mental life, its demonstration of the interaction of psychic and physical factors in illness and health, its description of neurotic and psychotic behavior patterns, and its analysis of the psychic mechanisms of "rationalization," "free association," "compensation" and the like—all these have passed into our common thought and speech. The general description which the psychotherapists give of the psychodynamic processes of growth toward or away from health and maturity has come to be widely accepted by many people who have no special knowledge of psychotherapeutic doctrine, as such. And the practical import of this new psychological outlook on human life may be noticed in almost every area of modern culture: education, legal theory, modern advertising and mass communication, politics and religion—in every area where interpersonal relations are primary and where people seek to direct human behavior toward preconceived human values. The influence of depth psychology upon modern art is axiomatic —and nearly as much can be said for modern music and literature. What was once a near-exclusive interest of the *avant-garde* in the arts has now become a staple element in current folklore: the comics, the video-drama, the "whodunit," the folksy magazines.

Moreover, the problem with which psychotherapy seeks to deal grows apace in modern life, a massive and tragic fact which touches and disturbs us all. The statistics of mental illness are notoriously elusive and unprecise, but they do point to an undeniable reality: the vast number of people whose health and well-being are drastically diminished because of psychic disorders of one sort or another, who in their maladaptation, make serious problems for themselves and society. The number of "psychiatric cases" in the United States—1945–49—has been variously estimated between ten and twenty million. Fishbein has concluded that half the population can be classed as neurotic and a third definitely require psychotherapeutic treatment! English studies show figures that are roughly parallel to these.[1]

Any knowledgeable pastor, or teacher, or social worker can produce testimony more vivid and poignant than these statistics. Who can move among his fellows in daily life without noting the signs of neurotic anxiety and hysteria, the invisible chains of compulsion and obsession, the dark unreason of paranoia, the wounds and scars of distorted and perverted living? How much unlived life there is—and maiming excess! How much cruelty and inhumanity wrought by men and women with sick souls, who try to justify themselves by appeal to the pious slogans of morality, patriotism and religion? The disorder of modern life is appalling in its spread and depth.

Psychotherapy has emerged as a significant help in identifying and measuring the dimensions of the neurotic pattern and its consequences in human life. The actual success of psychotherapy, thus far, has not been unqualified—and there are many reasons why the earlier hope of some, that psychotherapy was the new medical messiah, has waned. But, more than any other of the healing arts or the "sciences of man," psychotherapy has grappled with the problem of psychic health and disorder and has come to offer very great resources both for cure and prevention.

But psychotherapy has also become *more* than a healing art. It has gone on to develop normative theories of human growth and maturation. And because, for psychotherapy, interpersonal relations are primary, it has found itself confronted with questions about the human self and its wellbeing. As it seeks to deal with the disorders of the human psyche, it has found itself commenting on the great issues of human nature and the ordering of life. In the treatment of neurosis, the psychotherapist is inevitably brought face to face with the deeper problems which lie along the boundary between fact and faith, which involve not only psychodynamic processes but also the inmost and the utmost human concerns. Among the empirical sciences which study man, psychotherapy stands in a special relation to ethics, metaphysics and religion. Thus, what began as a clinical technique has acquired an extensive practical wisdom about human values and moves ahead to interpret the right ordering of life and the proper destiny of man!

It is inevitable, therefore, that thoughtful Christians should be deeply interested in psychotherapy and its import for Christianity. For Christianity has a common stake in the very same problems of human health and well-being. The Gospel began as a message about the fullness of human life in Christ and it has a long history of "the care of souls" and a ministry to the whole range of human needs and interests.[2] But the Christian *cura animarium* has always had to depend, for its psychological categories, upon the prevailing doctrines of each particular age through which the Church has passed. The psychological inadequacies which we can now so readily see in earlier ages are at least partially linked to the deficiencies in the secular psychologies which Christians borrowed and adapted to their uses in the service of humanity. The emergence of a new psychology is, therefore, of major importance to Christian teachers and ministers for it inevitably affects their interpretation of human relations and, above all, their practical dealings with persons in psychic distress. Modern psychotherapy has developed from and has contributed to a new depth psychology which, for all its defects and imperfection, is immensely superior to the traditional psychologies in its practical wisdom about human behavior and the making and remaking of human persons. And psychotherapy's attempts to pass beyond the level of practical wisdom to a *wisdom-about-life-itself* brings it even more closely into intimate encounter with the Christian wisdom and the Christian message.

It is quite natural, therefore, that psychotherapy and Christianity should find themselves related in both alliance and tension. An alliance is clearly indicated because of their common concern. The tension arises because of differences in basic perspective. And it is of great importance, in their respective future development, that the nature of this alliance and tension between the two be explored and appraised with full candor and explicitness. Are they allies? Are they rivals? What can the Christian minister or counselor appropriate from psychotherapy and how is he to judge what is compatible and incompatible with the Christian message? What are the basic issues about which current psychotherapeutic doctrine and authentic Christian teaching find themselves in conflict? What, in sum, are the terms of a fruitful alliance between psychotherapy and Christianity, in which both retain their true integrity and service to the truth? These are questions of vital importance to every thoughtful Christian—and they should be of *some* interest to the reflective psychotherapist, willing to examine the wider context of his work and thought.

It is common knowledge that a large and growing number of Christian pastors and counselors are turning to psychotherapy with avid hope of finding new resources for their own personal problems and for a more productive ministry to persons. The bibliography of books and articles on pastoral counseling grows faster than a man may read them—and to write still more is at least a rite of fellowship in a goodly company. But the vast majority of these essays are preoccupied with practical matters. From the Christian side, there has not been much critical examination of the basis of collaboration between psychotherapeutic doctrine and Christian thought.[3] From the side of psychotherapy, there are signs of interest in the applied uses of psychotherapeutic insight but very little inspection of the prior theoretical questions involved in any full-fledged collaboration with Christian ministers as colleagues in the service of humanity. One looks in vain among the standard books for knowledgeable recognition of the Christian message as a fruitful perspective for psychotherapeutic theory and practice.

It seems worth while, therefore, to undertake a further examination of the basic issues that lie between modern psychotherapy and the Christian message, and to evaluate the tendencies which make for alliance and rivalry between them. Psychotherapy is not a stable science, as the strife of its sects and systems plainly shows. There is even some difficulty in framing a general definition which will do justice to the competing claims of the divergent schools of psychoanalysis, to the wide variation in psychiatric theory and practice and to the confusion among the fringe groups which profess the power of mental healing. This is no proper place for a history of the general movement and I make no special claims to an exhaustive synoptic knowledge of the field.[4] But it is possible to see that all these groups form a common company of men and women seeking to understand and to repair human malfunction arising from mental and emotional disorder. Their proper datum is the living human person, in his quandary and his possibilities. And, for all the important differences between them in their theories and therapies, there are broad and general emphases which they all share, in sufficient degree, so that it is still legitimate to use the term "psychotherapy" in the singular.[5] There is, of course, something of the same sort of diversity among Christians, in doctrine, polity and practice. We shall not pause to analyze these differences, either, since it is enough for our purpose to keep in mind the basic shape and substance of the Christian message, as it can be related to this general problem of alliance and tension between psychotherapy and Christianity.

We shall begin by taking note of the positive contributions which the *practical* wisdom of psychotherapy offers to the thoughtful Christian, willing to submit to the necessary disciplines of study and guidance. Christianity ought always to be open to the enrichment of its practical programs by secular wisdoms of every sort; and it is abundantly clear that psychotherapy can be of immense value in this respect.

There are, as it seems to me, nine fundamental motifs of thought and practice which can be observed in all the schools of psychotherapy, which are particularly relevant to the Christian "care of souls" and crucial for a psychologically valid Christian view of man. We shall list these briefly and comment on their positive significance for Christian pastoral work. Our concern is mainly with ideas and not techniques, since it is by now an axiom in psychotherapy that a person cannot gain much in the way of technical proficiency, even as a lay counselor, by reading discussions of clinical procedure.[6] Rather, our object here is to analyze and evaluate the basic conceptions of psychotherapy and the Christian message, in order to estimate the terms of the alliance through which they may collaborate fruitfully with each other. It will be clear that the motifs thus abstracted from the practical wisdom of psychotherapy are not all new and most of them have decisive ethical and philosophical implications which reach far beyond their psychological import. Anyone familiar with the Judeo-Christian ethical tradition will readily recognize an ancestry for most of these motifs, older than modern psychology. And yet, psychotherapy has placed each of them in a new focus and has given to each a significantly new meaning which adds to its validity and applicability. And it is this new light on old ideas which the Christian may gratefully receive and appropriate for his own use in his understanding of and attitudes toward people—beginning with himself!

The *first* of the fundamental motifs is, of course, psychotherapy's constant stress on *respect for persons*. Psychotherapy is an authentic ministry to people in psychic distress and the large majority of psychotherapists are motivated by a high level of humane concern for their patients as persons in their own unique individuality and importance. The most crucial factor in therapy is the quality of the interpersonal relation between therapist and patient. Thus, the essential beginning of any treatment is the establishment of a permissive situation in which the person knows himself free to be himself and to be accepted and dealt with as himself. Rapport cannot be contrived; it must be achieved— and its chief prerequisite is a sincere and affirmative concern for persons, which is neither sentimental nor professional. But this requires that the therapist shall have come to be relatively secure in his own self-knowledge and self-respect; that he be capable of a nonexploitative regard for the patient. This means that sincere respect for others is not possible without self-respect, and vice versa. The therapeutic process gets under way only when the situation is free enough to stir the residues of freedom in the patient and candid enough to prompt him to self-revelation.[7]

There are, of course, wide differences among the therapists in their interpretations of this basic concept of rapport and concern for persons. Freud himself was a rather reserved man who tended to carry the older European habits of medical dignity and aloofness into the analytic situation. One of the analyst's chief roles was to serve as an umpire in the contest being played out between the ego versus the id and superego.[8] Thus Freud chose the now familiar technique of having the analyst out of sight of the patient on the couch.[9] Yet Freud laid great stress on the interpersonal relation between doctor and patient and consistently taught that the handling of the phenomena of "resistance" and "transference" was one of the most delicate and significant aspects of the therapeutic process. Some of the later therapists have altered the manner of the interview; it may be either face-to-face or with the doctor out of sight. Nowadays the stress is on a more fully mutual relation with the patient, with the therapist not so much as umpire as avowed friend and supporter.

> Nowadays, many psychiatrists no longer think of the therapist as unresponsive to and only a mirror of the patient's utterances. We consider him a participant observer in the psychotherapeutic process.[10]

But, in every case, it is the active concern for the patient as person which opens the door to effective therapy and keeps the process moving ahead.

The Christian minister may learn much from the psychotherapist in this matter of interpersonal relations. Most of us profess an earnest respect for persons but there are many who are not fully aware of their own need for valid self-knowledge in order to make their concern for others psychologically genuine. There is often the unsolved problem of the minister's own inner poise and self-esteem. He sometimes finds himself in a highly competitive professional situation in which his inner attitude toward himself and others may still be largely formed by ulterior interests. Thus, persons may appear to him as much means to his own ends as ends in themselves, even as he fulfills his professional role of one who comes "not to be served but to serve."[11] It is not easy to sort out the *persons* in a congregation, even if one knows their names and is familiar with their external situations. It is hard for a minister to separate his obligations to the individual-in-need from those which

he has to the group as a whole or to the larger institutional
context in which his work must be carried on. There is always the pressure for results in pastoral work which can be
more impressively reported in church statistics than in personal case histories. There is the ever-present temptation to
re-enforce one's self-esteem by courting the approval and
praise of one's admirers and to foster admiration as a remedy for inner insecurity and loneliness. And, finally, there is
the temptation to assume an authoritarian role, as minister,
priest or prophet, and to dominate the interpersonal relation by virtue of official status. We need very much to understand more fully, as the psychotherapist can show us
both by precept and example, what is actually required for
us to make our avowed *respect for persons* authentic and
productive.

But a *second* motif of psychotherapy reminds us of the
subpersonal and impersonal matrix of human life and insists upon the interpenetration of the biological and psychological vectors of life. No aspect of human experience
is beyond the conditioning action of the biological substrate
which we share with all living things. Bone of nature's bone
we are and flesh of nature's flesh. And the physical needs
and satisfactions of human life are integral parts of a whole
which, nevertheless, transcends the physical in ways unique
to man himself. It has offended many that psychotherapy
has stressed so much the pervasive influence of sex and
appetite, the need for physical satisfaction and the dangers
of frustration and privation. Others have rejoiced in what
they take to be license for a "scientific" hedonism. We shall

look at some of the issues posed by this general conception
for religion and ethics in later chapters. But even here we
can recognize the practical importance of this perspective
on human nature for the Christian care of souls.

It means that Christians must re-examine their traditional psychological ideas of "mind" and "body," of "spirit"
and "matter"—and take seriously the fact that the biblical
stress is on the wholeness of the self and the goodness of
created being insofar as it is what it was created to be. This
calls for a new understanding of the meaning of sex in God's
design for human living and a new estimate of the residue of
ethical and psychological dualisms which have come to
seem so self-evident in much of the Christian tradition.
Modern psychotherapy is the most powerful ally Christians
could find in the good cause of eliminating the hellenistic
and Gnostic conceptions of personality and spirit which
have so confused and obscured Christian ethics and metaphysics.

A *third* major motif in the practical wisdom of psychotherapy is its discovery that neurotic behavior is not really
meaningless and ought, therefore, never be dismissed as
simply weird or unintelligible. We have many residues
among us of the older notions of "possession" and "in-
sanity" and these tend to suggest to us that disoriented behavior and speech are literally non-sense. The psychotherapists can teach us better. They help us to see that neurotic
behavior has its own rationale; that it is an effort at communication as well as concealment, which may be bizarre
or obscure because of the protective distortions developed

as compensation for "normal" intrapersonal and interpersonal stability. The neurotic has long since lost the power to be fully candid with others, to be—himself! His security system is under pressure and threat—he fears rejection, disapprobation, nonsupport. Thus his growth line has been skewed and substitute patterns have come to regulate his communication with other persons, aimed at both disguise and disclosure. The ambiguity of his coded behavior is felt by the neurotic and it is a source of mixed satisfaction and frustration that others do not understand and respond appropriately. Psychotherapy is learning to make sense out of non-sense, in human words and actions—and to unravel the tangled skein of real reasons which make a neurotic pattern intelligible and, therefore, open to the kinds of insight which heal and restore. The physical symptoms of functional illnesses (e.g., conversion hysterias of all sorts) do not make much sense to the doctor who relies on physical diagnosis alone. But the psychotherapist has been able to show that physical symptoms are often clues to psychic disorder—and thus to account for many of the spectacular cures of "psychosomatic disease."[12] One of the primary assumptions of therapeutic practice is the actual intelligibility of the apparently unintelligible in human behavior—and the conviction that self-knowledge is the precondition of cure and health. From this follows the general idea that the basic enterprise in therapy is the quest for insight.

The import of this for Christian pastoral work is highly significant, for it affects one's attitude toward the people who do not readily fit the "normal" pattern. It is all too easy to be open to "like-minded" people and to be closed to the person who "doesn't fit" or whose behavior is "queer" by our measure of the normal. "I can't understand what's wrong with John" easily passes over to "I don't really *care* to understand him" or "Nobody can tell what he's up to." If we were persuaded by the psychotherapist, however, that human behavior can be understood, if we could learn to decode it, even a little, our attitude toward and acceptance of other persons would become significantly different and more productive. We could be both more patient and more determined in our effort at understanding others! And for this decoding, the psychotherapeutic description of neurotic types and symptoms is of great heuristic value. We should pray for deliverance, however, from the confident novice, who, with a smattering of theory, rushes in with ready-made diagnostic tags and labels—and thus treats persons as "cases." Neurotic behavior—or normal, for that matter—is not really understood until it is worked through and the emerging insights are honestly owned by the person himself. Self-knowledge is hard to come by, but there is no substitute for it.

A *fourth* motif has to do with the psychotherapist's conception of his function in the therapeutic process. I know no better summary of this than Fromm-Reichmann's chapter on "The Psychiatrist's Part" in her *Principles of Intensive Psychotherapy*.

What, then, are the basic requirements as to the personality and the professional abilities of a psychiatrist? If I were asked to answer this question in one sentence, I would reply,

"The psychotherapist must be able to listen." This does not
appear to be a startling statement, but it is intended to be
just that. To be able to listen and to gather information from
another person in this other person's own right, without re-
acting along the lines of one's own problems or experiences,
of which one may be reminded, perhaps in a disturbing way,
is an art of interpersonal exchange which few people are able
to practice without special training. To be in command of
this art is by no means tantamount to actually being a good
psychiatrist, but it is the prerequisite of all intensive psychotherapy.

The art of listening! How easy to speak of; how difficult
to practice! And the minister, being disposed to ready
speech, by training and profession, finds it very hard to
learn to listen, really listen. One can, of course, deliberately
keep his mouth shut, but this is not quite the same as listening and often the strain will show. Or, again, one may
find the other's story interesting because it stirs the memories of one's own problems and so reply, "I know how you
feel. I had a similar experience . . ." and then you're off
and running. We all know the definition of a bore: a man
who keeps on talking after we have thought of something
clever to say. Harry Stack Sullivan spoke of the therapist's
role as that of *participant observer*, one who is sufficiently
uninvolved in the case to hear and see the meanings of the
patient's communication but who is never content merely
to mirror them back or to accept them without interpretation. To listen means to be interested in *that person*; it
means to respond, not only in deep empathy but also in
intelligent dialogue. And most of all, it means having a

motive for hearing a person's story, which is derived from a conviction of the significance of *that* person and of *this* interpersonal relation. As we shall see, the Christian perspective supplies a further dimension to this relation with its presuppositions about the human self—but it might well concern us, first of all, that, in actual practice, Christian ministers often fail to *listen* and prefer to talk.

There is a *fifth* motif in psychotherapeutic doctrine which is of major significance to the Christian pastor or teacher. This is the general idea of the psychodynamic process of growth and development from infancy to maturity. Freud schematized this process with his theory of development from the oral, through the anal and phallic phases, to genital maturity, in which a person has become rationally adjusted to "reality" and capable of object love. Sullivan traces the successive stages of growth from primitive autism to mature and syntactic (rational) interpersonal relations. Fromm distinguishes between the immature "orientations" which are nonproductive, and the productive orientation which is characterized by self-acceptance and love of others. Though variously described, we can recognize the basic process of growth. The journey from infancy to maturity must traverse a maze and, whereas successful passage through any given phase contributes to the richness and stability of the growing person, failure at any given baffle means arrested development and distortion in the adult personality. Psychic maturity is, then, the end product of an incredibly complex process which covers the whole of life. Neurosis (or psychosis) is the product of a defective or deviant development. The growing self gets stuck, as it were, along the way and seeks to organize a substitutive, static system of self-and-other relations after the pattern of whatever phase of prematurity it had reached.

The implications of this hypothesis for understanding personal problems are manifold. It makes the conception of growth central, but it also rules out the notion of the *automatic* growth or natural unfolding of the self as though it were a seed or flower. Life is a precarious journey from birth to death, against initial odds and through successive crises which require, in advance, a measure of the maturity which successful passage of the crisis will produce. Every good teacher knows that one must treat young people as more mature than they are in order to help them become as mature as they may be.

For the Christian counselor this means that interpersonal relations are always in motion, toward or away from that sort of maturity in which a person has come to know, to accept and to *be* himself. It means that there are no final defeats and no final victories beyond which growth and process have no further relevance. Human life has always an open end and a growing edge. But this concept of dynamic growth also implies that one of the really crucial differences in human life lies between arrested development and true maturity. And this suggests that our real reliance must be on the power and the love which make for true maturity—and thus we find ourselves before the question of what *is* the ultimate source and substance of our well-being and well-doing.

There is a *sixth* psychotherapeutic motif which confronts the Christian counselor with both challenge and instruction. This is the general agreement that *moralism* is an invalid and harmful incentive to psychological maturity. From the beginning, Freud insisted that the therapist should refrain from forming or expressing moral judgments of praise or blame. This was not because the therapist had no moral judgments or was indifferent to moral values. Rather, the analytic process showed that the intervention of moralistic condemnation or exhortation was actually nonproductive of true moral growth and responsibility. There is a good reason for this. The invocation of duty and the appeal to the "ought" and "ought not" are, for the neurotic person, appeals to the borrowed and introjected value judgments of parents and society (the superego). Moralism is obedience to external and imposed moral force—mediated as though from within by a conscience formed largely by society and its surrogates. But true morality must come from the inner and freely willed value judgments of the self, in its power of self-acceptance and self-approval of the objectively right and good. Conventional morality is naturally moralistic and it normally represents a tyranny of the superego. This, say the psychotherapists, is inimical to authentic self-development, spontaneous moral insight and responsible freedom.[13]

There are many implications which follow from this rejection of moralism which affect our notions of Christian counseling, preaching and worship. A guilt-ridden person is apt to take the Christian counselor as a spokesman for customary morality; that is to say, a strong ally of his own superego. And since guilt feelings always point to a deeper moral conflict, the re-enforcement of the superego means a prolongation of the struggle or else an irrational solution of it. To be shocked and to condemn activates the other's conscience in such a way as to heighten the conflict. To reassure or approve reduces the tension. But neither really guides the person to the inner transformation which leads beyond guilt to faith and virtue.

As for preaching, one wonders how many sermons there are which are aimed at the superegos of the congregation, either to condemn or reassure without deep analysis of the ordeal of man's responsibility before God? How often is worship designed to rush up reinforcement to flagging moral endeavor, or to substitute propitiatory forms for the actual divine-human encounter?[14] How often are personal decisions sought and made—and also reported—which *appear* to represent a radical change in life, but from which the people fade back into the moral mediocrity which is all too normal for the life in our churches?

The fault here, in every case, is the confusion of moralism with authentic Christian ethics. It represents the domestication of Christianity in culture—and the identification of socially approved conduct and the righteous will of God. It is the effort to make a code by which men can measure themselves and others—and pronounce judgment! One might think it ironic that the psychotherapists should now teach Christians new reasons why an ethic of responsibility is superior to one of injunction and censorship—for it

was Jesus who transformed the moralism of *his* day into an
ethic which springs from the self in that true self-acceptance and self-assertion which is grounded in our love and
devotion to God.

A *seventh* general motif in psychotherapy's practical
counsel for Christians is its demonstration of the projective
and delusive character of much of our religious thought
and feeling. This is a disturbing and unwelcome thought to
some—and yet we can hardly deny the evidence that has
come to light in a multitude of psychotherapeutic case histories. They have shown, for example, how the mechanism
of "displacement" serves to transpose human attitudes of
fear and wrath, hostility and subservience from their original objects to other persons—and to God. A shrewd observer—a trained Christian counselor himself—ruefully
reports what many of us know: "Religion is a happy hunt-
ing ground for displacements!"[15] Psychotherapy has demonstrated the extraordinary frequency of mild anxiety neuroses and hysterias among the general population. From
this we might be able to see for ourselves how often the
conventional church experiences of such people either
maintain their neuroses *in statu* (with spurious grace to
"grin and bear it") or fail to aid them toward freedom and
maturity. There is a serious psychological hypocrisy in the
effort to "inspire" people whose inner self-systems are not
being changed; or to reassure anxious men and women by
optimistic pronouncements and a hearty program of un-
understood "religious activity." There is mortal danger in
the glib promises of peace and power through religion,

which do not involve the regeneration of a new life in
Christ Jesus and the remaking of society as a fit place for
God's children to live in, according to His will for brother-
hood and justice. It is well known that liberal Christianity
—especially in America—had a "social gospel," a prophetic
ethic which attempted the Christian criticism of society.
And yet have we not often enough observed the tragic paradox of the liberal churches of the upper middle classes ex-
erting what is actually a conservative tendency to resist
basic social reform because, at least in large part, they tend
to maintain people in a substitute formation of moralistic
anxiety and thus protect them from the deep searchings of
the Christian demand for depth regeneration and the real
renewal of society?

We may list an *eighth* common motif in modern psychotherapy which helps us to distinguish between the false
and authentic in religious feeling and decision. This is the
conception of *endopsychic conflict* and the ways in which
psychic energy can be locked up or reduced in the struggle
between the competing thrusts and controls of the unconscious. Psychotherapy helps explain why human beings ordinarily use only a small fraction of their potential energies
and powers in productive living. From it, we can learn why
fatigue and low-energy levels are more of a psychological
than physiological problem. The energy required to maintain censorship and control of unacceptable aggressive
drives has to come from the dynamic potential which might
otherwise be available for less inhibited enterprises. This
illuminates the plight of the rigid-normal person who lives

in fairly faithful obedience to his superego, doing most of the things he "should" and not many of the things he "shouldn't," but who still has no wholeness of health in him, because he is paying such an awful price of repression, desensitization and narrowed horizons of ethical experience —a pathetic diminution of the meaning and glory of human existence.

In this connection, psychotherapy helps us to see that in a culture like ours, the neurotic person *may* be in a somewhat more hopeful case than the rigid-normal. The latter has adjusted to a cultural setting which involves him in not only the conventional personal hypocrisies of business and society but also the massive, unintended brutalities of racial and economic injustice, rationalized and moralized by piety and patriotism. A man who has made his peace with this world and lives in psychic comfort in it is further from the Kingdom of God than the neurotic who, for all his disorder, may be in vital protest against the threat of superego "normalcy."[16]

Another corollary of this conception of endopsychic conflict is the need for discrimination in estimating the authenticity of religious feeling and belief. Psychotherapy has shown us the way in which wishful thinking confuses abstract ideals and concrete decisions, values emotion above reason and truth. It has shown us how the mechanism of projection helps explain neurotic religious belief—and neurotic unbelief! The therapist cannot, within his scientific premises, speak one way or the other about the reality of God, but he can warn us to distinguish between religious profession and religious performance—especially when religious professions issue in loveless and anxious living.

The last motif we shall mention is the most important of all: *the sovereign virtue of love* in the making and remaking of human persons. There is, of course, a wide variation in the analysis and interpretation of love but a common agreement that incorporative or possessive love is always inferior to outgoing concern for and loyalty to the well-being of the loved one. Thus, there is a stress upon the *quality* of love as decisive in human relations. The quality of the love which a growing child receives from the significant adults in his life is the most important factor in his development; the quality of love in the therapist or counselor is the most decisive factor in therapy;[17] the quality of love in a community of persons is the exact measure of its moral and spiritual health. Human life is the gift of love and the quest for love. Love cannot be wrested from life; it must be received as a gift and offered yet again as a gift to others. Psychotherapy has developed an impressive pile of evidence to show that the mass of human misery comes from the lack or the corruption of the love in their interpersonal relations —and an equally impressive demonstration that love is the chief restorative power in the remaking of psychic health and wholeness. At this point, psychotherapy challenges Christianity, which has always spoken of love to re-examine its psychological notions of love and to reconstruct its doctrine of the meaning and mode of object love among persons.

In these and in many other ways, modern psychotherapy

illumines the study of human behavior as nothing else can do and affords us a perspective which is indispensable to any human wisdom about ourselves. The aim of psychotherapy is self-knowledge, self-acceptance, self-expression. And, insofar as it reaches toward this aim, it becomes a most important ally for the Christian ministry to the whole man, in his health and salvation. This practical wisdom of psychotherapy raises questions for traditional Christian thought about man, insofar as this has been yoked with archaic psychological viewpoints, and provides many useful clues to the existential relations between faith and reason, belief and doubt, love and fear, freedom and bondage— and most of all, the complex question of productive interpersonal relationships. The modern Christian, be he pastor, teacher or interested layman, has a stake in the psychotherapeutic enterprise, and has both an obligation and an opportunity to explore its theories and to appropiate its practical wisdom.

But, from the very beginning, psychotherapy has been more than a practical wisdom. This was inevitable. In order to study human experience and its dynamic structures, some perspective on the human situation was required and some "model" of existence constructed. Modern psychotherapy emerged in a particular context and has developed along particular lines which have shaped its world view and made it into a *wisdom-about-life*, with basic convictions, or at least presuppositions, about the source and end and meaning of human life.

It has never been sufficiently noticed that, from Freud

on down to Fromm and Alexander, the men who have made psychotherapy were themselves heirs of a curious double legacy from the eighteenth and nineteenth centuries. On the one hand, they are direct descendants of the eighteenth-century "Enlightenment," that tremendous secular revolution against Christianity as it had developed in European civilization up to that time. Carl Becker[18] has told, in brilliant clarity, the story of how the deists and the rationalists of the eighteenth century—Voltaire, Diderot, Hume, Priestly and their company—undertook to refashion the ancient Christian dream of the city of God in heaven into a program for a heavenly city of man here on this earth. Their passionate aim and hope was the achievement of a good society, for men and by men, ordered by reason and energized by the ideals of liberty, equality and fraternity. Their basic credo can be summarized as follows:[19]

1. Man is not natively depraved.
2. The end of life is life itself; the good life on earth instead of the beatific life after death.
3. Man is capable, guided solely by the light of reason and experience, of perfecting the good life on earth.
4. The first and essential condition of the good life on earth is the freeing of men's minds from the bonds of ignorance and superstition (largely due to the benighted bond between Christianity and political tyranny).

The Enlightenment was by no means irreligious but it was, on the whole, profoundly anti-Christian. "Renunciation of the traditional revelation was the very condition of being truly enlightened," said one of these new humanists.[20]

"The basic idea of the Enlightenment," says Brinton, "is the belief that all human beings can attain here on this earth a state of perfection hitherto in the West thought to be possible only for Christians in a state of grace, and for them only after death."[21] The emancipation and education of mankind toward freedom and enlightenment became a powerful religious goal and incentive for moral effort. Posterity replaced God as judge and justifier of man's moral efforts and even the fierce butchers of the French Revolution (Robespierre in particular) were confident that a grateful later age would vindicate their inhumanity, justified because of its service to progress.[22] The men of the Enlightenment made a *religion* of reason and morality.

> For the love of God, they substituted the love of humanity; for the vicarious atonement the perfectibility of man through his own efforts; for the hope of immortality in another world the hope of living in the memory of future generations.[23]

Even a cursory examination of psychotherapeutic literature will show how deeply this secularist, humanist world view and commitment has entered into its outlook and main conceptions. For the most part, psychotheraphy's rejection of the Christian tradition is implicit but there are many eminent theorists and practitioners who have spelled out their humanist alternative to the Judeo-Christian tradition.[24] And it is a *gospel:* the good news that man can make for himself a good life—the best life there is for man. The typical psychotherapeutic discussion of the meanings and goals of life rests squarely on a doctrine of human autarchy

which insists on taking man not only as the measure of all
things but measurer as well!

But there was another great ideological development in
the nineteenth century which deeply affected the traditional conceptions of *nature* and man's relation to it. The
natural philosopher of the sixteenth and seventeenth centuries could interpret nature and man in the fashion of "the
new science" and still quite readily believe in God as
ground and source of nature; His purposive relation to matter and to human life seemed an evident and reasonable
article of faith.[25] This made possible a synoptic naturalism
which saw the world as a divinely ordered matrix of human
values and meanings and divine providence as a beneficent
and superhuman force working for the best ends of the
created order.

The impact of the developing sciences of physics and
biology produced an ominous change among some philosophers in their conception of nature and man's place in it.
Malthus and Darwin came to see nature as subpersonal and
irreducibly competitive. And Herbert Spencer built a
grimly reactionary but immensely popular social theory on
the "scientific" foundations of what he called "social
Darwinism." In Europe, Feuerbach and Vogt, Büchner,
Czolbe and Haeckel—all in their different ways—developed a *reductive naturalism*, in which God is ruled out and
human values are, in one way or another, unique emergents
in a natural process otherwise blind or indifferent to the human enterprise.[26] Man can and must make of nature what
he can; it is an illusion to suppose that nature is the created

organism in which God is working out His will and purpose.

Such a view of nature and man as an item in natural process is bound to stress the *instrumental* character of human reason and ideals. Mind is servant to vitality; reason is the tool of impulses far more primitive than logic and discourse. Conscious thought is shaped by logic and the pressures of social judgment; but libido lies below and leaps beyond the rational systems which men devise and the pious conventions by which they rationalize their affairs.

These two traditions of religious humanism and reductive naturalism had a common cause against the perennial philosophy and the Judeo-Christian tradition. Both agreed that life was the business of "man for himself" in a natural process with no supernatural reference beyond it. And it is this natural order which is the arena of human effort. Here —and nowhere else—can man seek to find the measure or the consummation of life's meaning.

Sigmund Freud was joint heir to both these traditions, and part of his authentic genius lay in the way he put the two together, maintaining all the while that he had no interest in the question of philosophical presuppositions or world view. Yet his discoveries of the nature of libidinal energy and his topography of the unconscious system of the mind have striking anticipations in the reductive naturalists who went before him. And always, for Freud, the processes of nature were amoral and nonpurposive. Nature is the casually ordered totality of mass and motion. It is an illusion to imagine that anything in nature corresponds to the human need for love and care; it is a delusion to suppose that there is anything "beyond" nature.[27]

Yet, on the other side, there was Freud's unswerving conviction that, within its natural limits, scientific reason could decode human behavior and, by its power, men could achieve for themselves the good life possible for man and enjoy it in moderation and fortitude. He was a devout believer in "progress" and trusted science as man's sole and sufficient source of valid wisdom.[28] And though he disavowed religion, there is a religious zeal in his sense of mission and service to humanity. In these respects, we can see the powerful residues of Enlightenment humanism at work in his system building.

The presuppositions of modern psychotherapy vary widely but, if we take the movement as a whole, we can see almost everywhere the formative influence of this complex inheritance of religious humanism and reductive naturalism, of secular liberalism and scientism. We shall be able to observe it when we explore the attitudes of representative psychotherapists toward personality and freedom, toward the human situation and the ordering of life, toward philosophy, ethics and religion. The modern pioneers in psychotherapy steadily maintained that they were quite neutral and quite empirical in their methodology—they believed they had no need of a philosophical context and supposed that they had none. But the merest backward glance shows how closely Freud allied his science with a definite metaphysical perspective: reductive naturalism and secular humanism. More recently, as later theorists have worked through the technical problems and have ventured further into the area of ethics and religion, this humanist, naturalist perspective comes to be more and more explicitly asserted and more and more tenaciously defended. Psychotherapy has grown up in the tradition of modern secularism and is one of its most important apologists in contemporary culture. Its primary focus and concern is man: man by himself in nature, man for himself in the world. It is no wonder, then, that psychotherapy, as a general movement with only a few exceptions, has been antipathetic or at least indifferent toward traditional Christianity.

The Christian who recognizes this context for tension and who is, nevertheless, still interested in appropriating the practical service of psychotherapy for the enrichment of Christian wisdom, must make a careful sounding of his situation. He must ask, in the first place, how closely tied to each other are the practical wisdom of psychotherapy and the secular tradition in which it has developed. If they are inseparable and mutually re-enforcing, then the conflict between psychotherapy and Christian faith is a serious one indeed—they are rivals. But if, instead, the connection between psychotherapy and this secularistic world view is adventitious, then the Christian could readily separate the one from the other—and "hold fast to that which is good."

It would seem obvious to the historian of ideas that the humanism and naturalism with which psychotherapy has, in the main, been associated is a quasi-religious faith—and an alternate faith to Christianity—which is not required, much less confirmed, by the scientific procedures and conclusions of clinical therapy. On the contrary, I believe, the Christian world view is not only a possible perspective for the psychotherapy of the future but a more adequate and valid one than any secularist faith can possibly provide.

It is one of the aims of this present essay to test these convictions by comparing these two faiths in some of the major areas in which they both have vital stakes. I wish to suggest that, while the *practical* wisdom of psychotherapy is a valid resource for the Christian care of souls, its humanist and naturalist *perspective* must be rejected. And from this thesis follows my basic proposal for the alliance between psychotherapy and Christianity: Let Christians gratefully receive the best psychotherapy has to offer, in clinical help and practical wisdom. Let us learn what they can teach, about human motivation and behavior, about the disorders and repair of psychic life—and make responsible use of what we learn, in good conscience and with disciplined understanding. But the Christian must stand firm on Christian ground, and not be overly impressed by claims that the *faith* of psychotherapy has the same scientific authority as its clinical axioms. This is simply not the case. Christians are enjoined "to bring all our thoughts captive to obey Christ," not in sacrifice of the intellect, but in freedom and unity of the Christian life shaped by the Gospel of Christ.

The Christian Gospel is a joyous word from God to man in the depths of his existence. It speaks of the origins and ends of human life, of God as ground and sustaining power of existence, of man under God's command and blessing, of man in quandary and sin, of God in Christ reconciling the world unto Himself, of the Holy Spirit making for a community of truly matured and fulfilled persons. It is a word of man's reliance on God, of man's hope in God, of God's imperative that we should love Him devotedly and our neighbors mutually. It is God's word by which He has ordered life from the beginning in faithfulness, has redeemed it in love and will so order it to His gracious end that men should be both righteous and blessed. The Gospel is a call to repentance and faith, new life and Christian maturity. It is a divine promise of reconciliation in a new fullness of life. It is an invitation of the Holy Spirit to life in the body of Christ, the beloved community of faith and grace, in which there spring up the spontaneous impulses to thanksgiving and worship and service to God, whose grace is the power of our goodness, whose service is our perfect freedom.

This, or something very like it, is the Christian *good news* to man in his disorderly wrestle with the bad news which his works and days bring forth. To those who believe it and who live by it, it furnishes a perspective on ultimates that sets in meaningful order the whole range of human experience. It is a wisdom about life and death and destiny, a singular and distinctive wisdom which is unique and final. And on these cardinal points of its proclamation, it makes for itself the tremendous claim of being true—really true—grounded in divine revelation and tested in human experience and history.

But the Christian Gospel is not the whole story of man's life upon the earth, nor does it properly pretend to be. It concerns itself with *ultimates*, with what matters most to

men if they are to find the meaning and the goodness and
the fulfillment of their existence. Yet *part* of God's purpose
in creating such a world as this, with man the unique creature in it that he is, was to produce a situation in which
human reason and decision count for something indispensable. This world is a life-setting where human wonder and
wisdom have an ample scope and place. The world, and all
things visible and invisible, are God's creation, for man's
discovery and understanding, for his tendance, use and enjoyment. It is man's proper business to seek wisdom about
himself and the world, to use his rational powers in the responsible freedom with which he is endowed by God Himself.

The Gospel is not, in this sense, a wisdom about the
world. It is neither a physics nor metaphysics; it is neither a
biology nor psychology. It judges all such wisdoms insofar
as they reach out toward life's final issues, but it cannot,
and ought not even to try, to direct the empirical sciences
within their own proper spheres of inquiry and method.
The Gospel, as a wisdom about life, must therefore always
be preached and heard in an intellectual context conditioned by human wisdom, as that wisdom seeks to form a
picture of the world and to achieve a cognitive understanding and control of nature, within limits not yet fully known.
The Gospel must be preached in the world to men in the
world, but it claims to have come from beyond the world
and to speak to men whose destinies lie beyond the world's
bounds. The Gospel is, therefore, always in a certain tension with the claims of these worldly wisdoms whenever

they pass beyond the orders of description and control and essay to speak of primitive and final truth about being and existence. This is an inevitable tension, since all truths are linked together in a continuum, and the discrimination between penultimate and ultimate truth is notoriously difficult. The Christian must take his wisdom about the world from the wisdom of the world. Yet at the same time he must judge this wisdom of the world by the Gospel's wisdom about life and its ultimate meaning. This is never an easy task, but it must be done; for the only alternatives are either to make over the Gospel into a secular wisdom (as, for example, the fundamentalists' rejection of biology or the liberal contention that there is something specific called "Christian economics") or else to take over one of the secular wisdoms as the gospel of life itself.

This relationship of the Christian wisdom about ultimates and the worldly wisdom about proximates is a complex undertaking, and it has had a most instructive history in the development of the Christian community and its relation to the human community. From the beginning, Christians have freely borrowed human wisdom and have sought to adjust truths of science and philosophy to the truths of the Gospel. But they have discovered always that there is a final incongruence between God's revelation and man's discovery. The Christian notices that human wisdoms always find themselves tempted to assert themselves as *the* gospel—the gospel of *human wisdom!* Over against the Christian teaching about God and man stands the secular account of man and man, in nature. This becomes the secular gospel—a joyous word that this discoverable world is the beginning and the end, and that man *is* the measure of all things. In this world, by his own faith and hope and wisdom, man can make a good life for himself. In one version or another this is the traditional *rival* gospel to high religion: the gospel of man's sufficiency, of man's final self-reliance.

Christians have often been tempted to set up a merely defensive antithesis to such a secular evangel and to claim for the Christian revelation the right of censorship in science and also the right of easy refuge in mystery in the face of the unknown or the theoretically inconvenient. Out of this reaction springs obscurantism, and like most security operations, it stifles the freedom of inquiry and it corrupts the judgment, both of faith and of reason. Men lose the liberty of the Gospel when they are driven into a phobia of human wisdom—just as we equally lose the wisdom and the power of the Gospel when we base our highest hopes upon the wisdom of the world.

All the main epochs of the Church's life have had their characteristic challenge from contemporary, secular wisdom. In the ancient Church it was the problem of a metaphysical outlook appropriate for the Christian affirmations. That struggle saw the failure of both extreme solutions to the problem, and from it there finally emerged the maturing of a Christian instinct for judging the world's wisdom. In the Middle Ages, the challenge came from the new science of the Arabs and of Aristotle. The resolution of this conflict was much less decisive. By the end of the fifteenth century, the relation of revelation and reason was badly confused and unsettled. The Protestant Reformation set out to separate the Gospel from human wisdom, but then, because of its pervasive anti-intellectualism, it could not find a way to put them back together again in fruitful interaction. Meanwhile, the Renaissance was projecting the vision of a new city of earth to rest on the footings of the new sciences and philosophy. As for Rome, after the Council of Trent, it sought to maintain the old, medieval hieratic order of dogma, truth and priesthood, in which science can exist only in a servile and submissive role. Finally, when the forces of enlightenment and revolution shattered the old order in European culture, Christianity found itself challenged by the new sciences of man, and their implications for a human estimate of the human situation. Modern science has already behind it tremendous achievements and has acquired immense prestige in the modern world. Christianity has been forced into the ideological defensive, before the growing confidence that the "other gospel" of "man for himself" is the true gospel. This "other gospel" claims to be not only compatible with science but derived from and established by science. This rivalry and clash of rival gospels constitutes one of the most massive and urgent issues before the Christian thinker in our time. One salient fact stands forth in this new crisis which knowledgeable Christians should recognize as an old dilemma: Christians must seek to understand the world they live in by the standard methods of empirical inquiry, and they must also judge their worldly wisdom by the final wisdom of the Gospel.

Christianity must seek alliance with valid human wisdom, and it must at every point resist the rivalry of every merely human gospel.

Psychotherapy constitutes a prime instance of just such a practical wisdom which modern Christianity needs and can appropriate—associated with a humanistic world view which Christianity must reject. Christianity and psychotherapy are both concerned with the well-being of the whole human person. And this concern leads them both to questions and conclusions about basic issues in human existence and destiny. Psychotherapy moves toward the borders of religion and Christianity moves toward the borders of the healing arts. There is need for an alliance between the two, based on a careful and candid analysis of the tensions which also exist between them. It is important to define some of the basic issues in this tension and to explore the possibilities of their resolution. This will be the task before us in the following chapters. Here we may outline the questions which require discussion.

The first, and constant, question is the clash of first principles as to the reality and the nature of God. As an empirical science, psychotherapy has neither more nor less to say about the reality of God than does biology or astronomy. But the psychotherapist, as a man deeply involved with other men in the widest and deepest concerns of life, is bound to have assumptions and presuppositions about the ultimate reach of existence. He will believe that the natural order is self-contained and self-intelligible or that it is not. He will see man as the measure of all things, or he will not.

And either way, he should recognize that the difference between theistic faith and religious humanism is categorical; even the agnostic tends to commit himself one way or the other, sooner or later. The Christian Gospel does not depend upon a given physics or psychology—save by an illicit extension of its revelational principles. But it does stand or fall by its belief in God—Creator, Redeemer, Consummator—and in the totality of existence as derived from and dependent on Him. Are psychotherapists bound to deny this faith, or to hold it in disjoined relation to their science? To answer this question requires a deliberate and thorough examination of the relation between basic faith and a man's world view. Professor Seward Hiltner, who has done much to show how the practical wisdom of psychotherapists applies to the tasks of Christian counseling, has rightly suggested that they need to go further to develop "the intrinsic intellectual aspects of their own discipline."[29]

> Because of its very nature, being existential as well as scientific, psychotherapeutic work should beget a theory which has philosophical, and perhaps even theological, implications. To be adequately rooted in the whole fabric of human knowledge, it needs to explore a wider context than has usually been done. As it is we are only now beginning to have work done on psychotherapeutic theory which is also well versed in the thinking of modern philosophy and philosophical aspects of the sciences in general. Such work is just as important, and ultimately as valuable in a practical sense, as is detailed scientific investigation of limited areas.

A second issue which lies between the two wisdoms is the basic idea of the human self and its freedom. Insofar as it remains an empirical science, psychotherapy must operate within the limits of its phenomenological description of human systems of behavior. But, in a theory which stresses so strongly the relations of persons, it turns out to be impossible for the therapist to disguise his extraempirical assumptions as to the inner nature of personality. Christian faith is not necessarily tied to any given psychology, but it stands or falls by its belief in the reality of the individual self, as a discrete and finite entity, characterized by unique capacities for freedom, faith and love, in communion with God. Psychotherapy has, on the whole, left this issue to be settled more by negative implication than analysis; but occasionally we find an explicit and disparaging dismissal of the idea of the human self as a finite entity.[30] We shall look more closely into this whole question in the next chapter.

The other main issues we shall undertake to examine are (1) the human quandary (sin), (2) the human possibility (salvation), and (3) the ordering of life (ethics). In respect of each of these unavoidable concerns of any human wisdom we shall compare the general notions to be found in representative psychotherapeutic theorists with the Christian message—and endeavor to suggest where they clash and how they could be joined in fruitful synthesis.

Even in advance of this more detailed examination, we can set down the general terms in which we can conceive of an alliance between psychotherapy and Christianity which would maintain the integrity of each and keep open the way to mutually useful collaboration. The Christian doctrine of man, if it is to be authentic, must be a prime corollary of the Christian faith in God as Creator and Redeemer. It must interpret human existence in terms of finitude and freedom. It must plumb the full depth of the human quandary and identify the tragedy of sin as well as the harm wrought by error. It must see the human possibility as radically dependent upon the grace and power of God in Christ, reconciling the world unto Himself. It must place man's claim to wisdom and controlling knowledge under the higher order of God's self-disclosure as Lord and Savior. It must seek for the ordering of life through God's righteous rule and redemptive grace, manifest in Jesus Christ.

It should go without saying that no professional psychotherapist would have to believe all this in order to pursue his practical business; and certainly these are not questions to be raised in the consulting room. But if he rejects them in his own mind, if he construes his basic theory in antithesis to them and claims the authority of his science for his philosophical and religious ideas, we have then a serious rival to the Christian faith. This rival gospel may seek to become a cult: the model of "the religion of the future." But, in this case, the invocation of science will be inadmissible and faith must compete against faith. Christianity can, and ought to, learn from every human wisdom which, for its own part, will allow for the Christian perspective as a legitimate context of interpretation. Christianity exceeds its rights when it seeks to direct or coerce a process of inquiry which respects its own proper limits. But it is entirely justified in demanding that the examination of first principles be conducted in the temple court of faith and commitment, and not be misrepresented as having been settled in the laboratory and the clinic.

In the alliance I propose between psychotherapy and

Christian pastoral care, the Christian message will claim to be the measure of valid wisdom about the ultimate questions men ask concerning their own existence. Psychotherapy may rightly claim to be both teacher and judge and the effective means of repair and guidance of human behavior. We have tried to indicate something of what the thoughtful Christian may learn from this practical wisdom and we acknowledge that this learning is bound to affect the form and content of many of the traditional notions of Christian thought. By the same token, it seems to me reasonable that at least some psychotherapists ought to be willing to learn from the Christian wisdom new premises and implications for their own understanding of the psychodynamic process. Laboring thus together, the believing psychotherapist and the well-furnished Christian counselor could serve us all in ampler wisdom and greater effectiveness.

In some such way as this, psychotherapy can be yet another—the latest, and perhaps the most significant thus far —of the epochal developments of human wisdom to be gratefully appropriated in the service of Christian living. Thus we might all share in the process by which we are enjoined to "attain to the unity of the faith and of the knowledge of the Son of God, [to come] *to mature manhood,* to the measure of the stature of the fullness of Christ. . . . Speaking the truth in love, we are *to grow up in every way* into him who is the head, into Christ."*[31]

* Scriptural quotations are from *The Revised Standard Version of the New Testament,* copyright, 1946, by the Division of Christian Education of the National Council of the Churches of Christ in the U.S.A. Published by Thomas Nelson & Sons.

CHAPTER TWO

The Human Self and Its Freedom

Freud "discovered" America in 1909 when he came to Worcester, Massachusetts, with Jung, Ferenczi and Ernest Jones to present the new theories of psychoanalysis to a select academic company celebrating the twentieth anniversary of Clark University.[1] The general reaction to the presentation was not especially favorable, but Freud made one distinguished American convert who greatly affected the subsequent progress of psychotherapy in America. This was James Jackson Putnam, professor of neuropathology at Harvard. Putnam attended the Worcester lectures, became convinced that Freud's discoveries confirmed and extended some of his own psychiatric ideas and proceeded to adopt and to advocate the new psychology. His personal prestige (in Boston the Putnams spoke to both the Lowells and the Cabots!) and his eminence in the scientific world of America made him one of the most effective sponsors the psychoanalytic movement could have found in this country.[2] But even as an ardent champion and practitioner of psychoanalysis, Putnam had certain reservations and misgivings which he felt bound to express. He was deeply convinced that the Freudian clinical theories required a wider philosophical and ethical orientation than the master had allowed. On May 10, 1911, Putnam read a paper to the American Psychopathological Association entitled, "A Plea for the Study of Philosophic Methods in Preparation for Psychoanalytic Work"; the following September he read a similar essay to the Third Congress of the International Psychoanalytic Association at Weimar. Yet, despite the fact that he was held in high regard among the Freudians because of his support in America and his holding the line against the defections of Jung and Adler, none of the leaders in the movement paid the slightest attention to Putnam's demand for a philosophical perspective for this new scientific enterprise.

Four years later Putnam returned to the problem with a paper on "The Necessity of Metaphysics," in which he reviewed the thesis that psychoanalysis would be a richer and more valid science if it took into account the prior questions which clustered around its fringes and which had been, up to that time, either ignored, or settled by assumption. Finally, in his very last—and unfinished—essay, he sought to assess the "Elements of Strength and Elements of Weakness in Psychoanalytic Doctrines."[3]

From the very first, Freud and his colleagues rejected Putnam's proposals as "an impossible demand," as "only another tyranny, even though disguised by the most honorable motives."[4] In a grateful preface to Putnam's posthumous *Addresses on Psychoanalysis*, Freud comments on

Putnam's concern about the wider context of psychoanalytic thought:[5]

> So it is not to be wondered at that a mind with such preeminently ethical and philosophical tendencies as Putnam's should have desired, after he had plunged deep into psychoanalysis, to establish the closest relation between it and the aims which lay nearest his heart. But his enthusiasm, so admirable in a man of his advanced age, did not succeed in carrying others along with him. Younger people remained cooler. It was especially Ferenczi who expressed the opposite view. The decisive reason for the rejection of Putnam's proposals was the doubt as to which of the philosophical systems should be accepted, since they all seemed to rest on an equally insecure basis, and since everything had up till then been sacrificed for the sake of the relative certainty of the results of psychoanalysis. It seemed more prudent to wait to discover whether a particular attitude towards life might be forced upon us with all the weight of necessity by analytical investigation.

For the same book, Ernest Jones (the pioneer Freudian in Britain) wrote an "Obituary," in which he praised Putnam as physician and scientist—and foremost American advocate of psychoanalysis! But his comment on Putnam's philosophical interests is quite revealing:[6]

> He [Putnam] maintained that it was highly desirable, if not absolutely essential, to widen the basis of psycho-analytical principles by incorporating into them certain philosophical views, especially concerning the relationship of the individual to the community at large and to the universe in general. He regarded this, not as criticism of psycho-analysis, but as a proposed enrichment of it. . . . On this matter

alone, which evidently meant a great deal to him personally, he was really obstinate, and he could never be brought to see how it could be possible to take the results of psycho-analytical investigations quite empirically without feeling the need to commit oneself to any particular philosophical system. For years he maintained a steady correspondence with me on this question, and it was a genuine disappointment to him that his views made so little impression on his psycho-analytical colleagues.

What were Putnam's proposals? Principally, that therapists face the questions about the nature of the human self and its freedom, the quality of the human good and its realization, the reality and relevance of high religion and the limits of a naturalistic methodology for the full interpretation of human existence. Although he was himself an idealist (a close friend of Royce and Bowditch), he was not doctrinaire as to the specific mode by which his program should be carried out—his only insistence was that the effort be made to get beyond the empiricism and naturalism which he recognized as then characteristic of the movement. "The primary requisite, however, is that we, as physicians, should ourselves have these principles in our minds, for without them we cannot do adequate justice in thought to our patients' deepest cravings and intuitions. Without them, we cannot even explain our own cravings and intuitions. . . ." And these basic "principles"? Putnam lists four:[7]

1. The transcendental reality of the self.
2. The spiritual origin and destiny of the self.

3. The orientation of the self to an enlarging good which is real.
4. The ethical obligations of love and aspiration.

Putnam was brushed aside and his story has been nearly forgotten, even among the psychotherapists. But it serves as an excellent illustration of a persisting difficulty in any honest and productive alliance between psychotherapy and Christianity. We have already seen that psychotherapy did, in fact, develop in an atmosphere conditioned by the reductive naturalism and secularism of the nineteenth century. Freud claimed that all philosophic systems are equally uncertain and Jones appears to have believed that all the basic issues could be settled "quite empirically"! Putnam's obstinate demand was a sort of personal crotchet, allowable in an otherwise valued ally—but not to be taken seriously! Yet all the while, they were themselves working in a context which simply had no place for Putnam's "principles." They declined the philosophic enterprise because they already had a philosophic outlook which had come to be taken so for granted that all contrary philosophical possibilities were ignored, *by not being seen as possibilities at all!* Socrates' dictum about the unexamined life applies to perspectives as well.

The problem still remains. We may stand on very different philosophic ground and yet renew Professor Putnam's essential proposal. Psychotherapy deals with the living human person, in his experiences of disorientation and reorientation as a person. And what *is* a person and what is the meaning of selfhood and agency? Does the therapist avoid

having some conception of, or at the very least, some pre-
supposition about the nature of personality? It may be clear
or vague, it may be formulated or undefined—but it will be
there and it will affect the inner quality of his interpersonal
relations. One's doctrine of the self may be held with the
utmost tentativity or dogmatism, it may represent any one
of several traditions of thought—but it cannot successfully
evade the issue. Any basic wisdom about human life entails
some sort of a notion of the human self, as the agent of human action and the focus of human behavior. Beyond any
of the other "sciences of man" or any other of the branches
of medicine, psychotherapy finds itself confronted with this
problem of the nature of the self. The therapist's relation
to his patient turns more crucially upon the validity of his
concept of the person than does, say, surgery or anthropology. Thus far, it must be reported, psychotherapy, by and
large, has not fully faced or amply settled this crucial issue.
Yet any alliance between psychotherapy and Christian
thought must inevitably turn on the way in which such a
question as this is dealt with.

There is a disenchanting history of reflection on this
topic. Of all the great recurrent themes of metaphysics, the
nature of personality has been probably the least illuminated by the *philosophia perennis*. The ancients thought
more readily and wisely of Man than they ever did of individual persons. For Plato, the individual is significant as he
participates, more or less, in the pattern of humanity, which
alone is real and identical for all men. Aristotle emphasized
the unity and the permanence of the human species, in

which individuals come to be and pass away. Thus Gilson is right, I think, in his comment that, for the Greeks, "in the long run the individuals, as individuals, do not count."[8] The Christians had no developed metaphysic to substitute for this Greek view, but they did have their biblical heritage which insisted upon the subsistence and the originality of each individual human self—and then they tried to match their message and their metaphysics.[9]

For the Christian, the problem of the self has been closely joined to the problem of the personality of Jesus Christ. It was in his effort to find the way between the extremes of Nestorius and Eutyches that Boethius framed the definition of a person which became classical for the medieval schoolmen: "A person is an individual substance of a rational nature."[10] Both Aquinas and Scotus insisted on the singularity, dignity and permanence of the human person and they maintained, in common, the essential Christian demand that every psychology make a place for the human self as distinct from every other, as "an original source of rational activity responsibly deciding his own future destiny."[11] Still, the medieval psychology was not ripe for development into an adequate empirical study and the modern philosophers who followed Descartes' lead in separating body and mind were never quite able to unite them in an authentic whole.[12]

Immanuel Kant gave the problem a decisive fresh beginning but he had started up so much other game that his toilsome deduction of the relation between the empirical and the transcendental self has hardly yet got its due and proper notice.[13] The efforts of the "philosophical psychologists" of the nineteenth century to develop an introspective method of study of the self proved heuristically barren.[14] In spite of all that had gone before, the traditional stereotype of what E. S. Robinson used to call "the little-man-in-the-head" concept of the soul dominated both the academic and the popular thought against which Freud and the pioneers of modern psychotherapy were understandably in revolt. This legacy they were determined to get rid of in order to have a clear look at the phenomena of human behavior and the phenomenology of the human self.[15]

The new psychologist, therefore, abandoned the philosophical inquiry about personality and the self in favor of the empirical study of human behavior. And there is no denying that this was an enormously productive transformation of the whole psychological enterprise. It has yielded new studies of man as "an irritable organism" (Fenichel) and from this we have gained significant knowledge of the processes of perception, learning, reflex and conditioned behavior of various levels—and, not least of all, we have come to understand more concretely our firm rootage in the order of animate nature. At another level, the new psychology has undertaken to *observe*, as from without, the relation of man to his congeners and, from this, to describe, as though objectively, how the human organism interacts in the complex process of social relations. This has produced a wealth of new knowledge in the opening fields of social psychology, sociology and anthropology. But above and beyond these levels of observation and interpretation, psychotherapy has gone on to explore the inner, psychodynamic patterns of human growth and development, retardation and deviation. From this exploration has come the practical wisdom about the facilitation of personal development and the repair of aberrations. All this has afforded us a new picture of the career-line of the human organism from conception to death and has given us a picture of man as agent and reagent in a constant flux of stimuli and responses which are conditioned by society and culture, by particular circumstance and personal history, but still amenable to scientific analysis, prediction and control. The contribution thus rendered to modern man's self-knowledge and social understanding is immense, and the debt we owe is gratefully acknowledged by all save those who demand that the findings of the positive sciences be dictated by preconceived dogmas.

With this phenomenological description of human behavior and the human being in action, the Christian has no proper quarrel. From it he can learn much—more than he could from the descriptive sections of the older psychologies. His questions arise, however, when the empiricists and the naturalists assert, or clearly imply, that man is *nothing but* the sum of the energy systems so described, and when it is declared that the old problem of the transcendental self is meaningless.[16] When an eminent psychotherapeutic theorist pays patronizing tribute at the interment of the dead notion of the soul, the Christian in the audience might feel entitled to a question whether the death was due to "natural causes."

I must pay tribute to the soul even as I desert her for she is of ancient and noble lineage. For many, belief in the soul is intertwined with their loves and hopes and aspirations. But in this theory I am about to outline she has no place and no function.[17]

Ockham's razor is still a necessity for the well-groomed theorist but it must be wielded with some care and gentleness. The judgment that a given idea is superfluous requires that all the significant data under consideration be explained by another and simpler hypothesis which is itself free from contradiction. If Mullahy means by "soul" the basic nexus of the singularity and transcendental reality of the human self, then he also means that his theory will account for *all* significant human experience which has been thought by some to suggest such an idea—and do it at least as exhaustively as any alternate theory which does refer to the category of the transcendental self. And does Mullahy's theory do this? A fair number of people, moderately competent to follow and assess an argument, are not convinced.

For one thing, no empiricist theory of interpersonal relations adequately accounts for the differences between inter*personal* relations and, say, inter*equine* or inter*apic* relations! Are not such differences real and must they not have an adequate accounting? We may observe and describe person-to-person relations. We may also observe and describe person-to-*porcine* relations. And we will note and interpret the similarities in both types of relations. But what of the differences? Persons and pigs are like and unlike— and it is the unlikeness which Mullahy and Sullivan and the empirical psychologists do not fully explain. It is simply ambiguous to hold that these observable differences are matters of degree—for when *are* differences, differences of degree and differences of *kind? This* is the question!

In the second place, the psychological concept of the self as a system of biological energies shaped by social forces brings us back around to the ancient concept of the individual as an instance of a universal type of psychic organization. And against this the same complaint is just that the singular individual, as an individual, does not count in the long run. A person as an episodic organization of biological vitality and social influence—this notion exalts the process at the expense of the idea of the singular self.

The idea of the soul had its faults; but, on its own proper terms, it provided a partially intelligible account of the differences between persons and other animate organisms and it did secure the singularity of the individual self as the chief mark of man's significance and worth.

The naturalistic, humanistic view of the self illustrates the basic clash between its whole world view and that of Christianity. For the "medical-naturalist" like Freud or the cultural-naturalist like Sullivan, the doctrine of the "psyche" or the self is not only independent of the idea of God; it is another aspect of the denial of the idea of God. Such a self naturally exists in a natural process in which nature itself is the self-subsistent. Thus, the secular world view proves highly compatible to a reductionist view of the person—and incompatible with the Christian outlook.

The Christian cannot fit this naturalist view of the person into his Christian perspective. The Gospel does not specify or elaborate an empirical psychology or metapsychology and thus the Christian is free to adopt validated practical wisdom from any quarter. Nor has the Christian wrestle with metaphysics provided a conclusion which settles the hard questions of body-mind, causality-freedom, time-eternity, questions which are bound to disturb any serious reflection in this area. In the history of Christian thought there have been widely divergent views of the self as between Tertullian and Origen, St. Thomas and Duns Scotus, Erasmus, Luther and Jonathan Edwards. Indeed, one could fairly say that the doctrine of the self is still one of the seriously unsettled areas in contemporary Christian thought—an urgent challenge to the ongoing tasks of philosophical theology.[18]

But the Christian message does entail certain specific notions which have to be fitted into empirical psychology which is then to be assimilated into the Christian wisdom. Each human self is a unique creature of God. He is known and loved of God—and his selfhood is just precisely the mode of his relation to God, in being, knowledge and love.[19] He is fully involved in the natural order, yet he passes beyond the limits of that order through his participation in the transcendental unities of reason, freedom and grace. To be a man is to be a unique entity, not merely an instance of a process or a species; a singular existent capable of being known as a self and of knowing other selves—but always in a transcendental relation to God, who stands before and beyond our existence as the *ground* of our existence whether as organisms or as persons.

To be a human self means to live in memory, faith, freedom—and never to be subsumed fully within the causal (empirical) order. It is to share in the creative and redemptive processes in which God is working, with unwearied respect for man's freedom. It is to have one's own part in the divine enterprise of maturing the singular selves which He has made—to glorify and to enjoy Him (and the richness of being) forever! In the depths of his being, man is radically dependent upon the power of God. In the height of his being, man is beloved child and "image" of God: the finite creature made for communion with his Creator.

Such a self is a unique existent, perdurably distinct from every other being, related to every level of creation and to the Creator—but not subsumed under any or all the processes in which he participates. In the vast web of physical, biological, psychological and sociological patterns in which he is caught up, man may be described in strict commensuration with other data of the same sort. But none of these nor all of them together denote man's essential and distinctive being. For the man who can describe himself *in* nature transcends the nature thus described by the very power of the knowledge which validates his description. Man's self-knowledge is, likewise, the measure of his self-transcendence. Only in relation to God is there no transcendence, for our knowledge of God is not the knowledge of an *object* (i.e., of a member of a class). It is, rather, our knowledge of

God's knowledge of *us* (i.e., His self-disclosure, or revelation). In the Christian view, therefore, there could be no human selves apart from God—without a relation to God —because the ground or anchor point of the self's transcendence is in God. In no other way could a finite self subsist transcendently. If God is not, the unique self is not. And, conversely, the denial of the reality of the singular self is a stage on the way to the denial of God.

To be a self, in Christian terms, is to exist in a unique relation to God: in every way dependent upon God, yet at every point open to the options and crises which arise in life situations in which we come to be, and come to be ourselves, in our knowledge of other selves and of God—and our being known by them. It is the life of interpersonal action and responsibility, with our fellows and with God—in faith or unfaith, in conflict or harmony, hostility or love, tragedy or blessedness. The Christian perspective on selfhood is radically theocentric: man from God, man before God, man against God, man redeemed by God, man in communion with God, in and through the God-man.

The Christian does not ask the psychologist to accept the Christian faith nor demand that his empirical view of the human person-in-action resonate with all the basic ideas of the Christian message. He ought, in fact, to be suspicious of *any* attempt to *describe* or to *locate* the self. Any such description would imply that the self is subsumable under the causal order of nature. But it is axiomatic that the self is not a perceptible object—and cannot be! The Christian, then, maintains only his basic requirement: that the self be interpreted as singular and subsistent. What he rightly complains of is the naturalistic contention that the self can be exhaustively defined in reductionist terms and the Christian idea excluded by the law of parsimony. For example, "Personality as a historic whole should be defined as *the entire sequence of organized governmental processes in the brain from birth to death.*"[20] The Christian is not disposed to deny such a proposition; he can recognize its genuine heuristic merit. But what *more* is there to be said for the self? Is the person *nothing more* than the sum of the energy systems, integrated by the brain? This clearly is not an exhaustive, or final answer, for even the tyro in metaphysics will know that the relation of brain and mind is not a simple correlation.

Actually, of course, the psychotherapists have wrestled with some of the implications of this problem and have sought to make intelligible the synthesis between their empirical knowledge and their world view. They, too, live by their faith. It is faith, of one sort or another, which launches and guides all inquiry; and yet faith, in turn, is affected by the outcome of the inquiry. If the psychotherapists have been guided largely by a naturalistic, humanistic faith—and if their faith has guided their presuppositions and conclusions about the ultimate—then we may understand the conflict between the Christian notion of person and the naturalist view of person as a quarrel *between believers*, and not an unequal battle between a camp of wan fideists and an army of robust scientists. And there is one more consideration: we may rightly ask which of the two

views of man gives the richest and truest base for the psychotherapeutic enterprise? The process of therapy is an affair between persons. Is not the effect and residue of such a
process conditioned by the ideas which these persons have
about themselves, and each other—and God? May we not
reconsider Putnam's old contention, with new relevance
and point: without some considered theory of the self, we
cannot do justice to the deepest cravings and intuitions
which we see in others, or in ourselves?

We have seen that the psychotherapists began by dis-
missing "the little-man-in-the-back-of-the-head." They have
shown us, with greater concreteness and clarity than any
previous psychology, how the human self *emerges* in a biological process, how it *grows* in a societal matrix, and how it
depends on both the processes at every point and is affected by them at every level. They help us to see the career
line of the individual as a series of impulsions, in each of
which he is thrust out of the near-equilibrium he may have
gained in the preceding phase. Growth is incalculably forward, into new phases and stages, always fraught with risk
and hope. Birth is an impulsion which *individualizes* the
organism and thrusts it into a new adventure of separate-
ness-and-dependence. Freud's notions of oral, anal and
phallic phases are an insightful way of interpreting the
process by which biological vitality acquires form and then
breaks through the forms acquired in its drive toward genital maturity. The Oedipal situation (viz., the child's possessive attachment to parents) precipitates another crisis
and a new impulsion toward the *socialization* of the indi-

vidual. Sullivan has a wonderfully perceptive summary of the significance of this impulsion beyond the family. He calls it "the quiet miracle of preadolescence":[21]

> I say "miracle" of preadolescence because now for the first time from birth, we might say even from conception, there is a movement from what we might, after traditional usage, call egocentricity, toward a fully social state . . . one begins to feel human in a sense in which one has not previously felt human. One becomes more fully human in that one begins to appreciate the common humanity of people—there comes a new sympathy for the other fellow. . . . In other words, the feeling of humanity is one of the aspects of the expansion of personality which comes in preadolescence.

The self-system develops further. Childhood is ended by the onset of puberty, which is yet a third major impulsion of the self into a radically new self-orientation and new patterns of interpersonal relation. Psychotherapeutic theory has tended to neglect somewhat the rich and positive significance of self-development and humanization in adolescence. This is doubtless due to the early preoccupation with infantile motivation and regression in the background of neurosis. Still, the psychodynamic development of adolescents is one which calls for freshly conceived exploration. The results would, I believe, do much to alter our traditional notions of secondary and college education, of courtship and marriage—and above all, vocational decision and preparation.

Beyond adolescence there opens the successive psychobiological phases of adulthood, menopause and senescence.

Psychotherapy has not probed as fully as it might into the dynamic possibilities of self-development and self-expression in these phases—and has not done as much as it doubtless will to demonstrate empirically the patterns by which the modern adults can gain and keep their sanity, in dignity and freedom and social significance.

But even now the outlines of the psychotherapeutic picture of the self have become clear. The self emerges in and is formed by this obstacle course of life. It is the self-registering index of the success or failure of the human organism in negotiating the hurdles and the maze. The central focus in this idea of the self appetency: the thrust of the individual toward the environment in need and desire. The self is shaped by the ends toward which it drives and the means adopted to the ends.

Freud developed his "metapsychological topography of the mind" as a kind of myth of the self, both in its emergence and structure. The primal center of the self, for Freud, is what he called the id; this is the hedonic drive (*Lust-Unlust Prinzip*) which aims at nothing but discharge of tension, and homeostasis. This basic form of energy is relatively constant, uneducable and quite amoral; Fenichel speaks of it as a "core of a dynamic, driving chaos of forces, which strive for discharge and nothing else."[22] But the organism cannot survive unless its heedless desires are curbed and patterns of constraint and direction are set up. In the human self, these inhibitory and directive patterns come from two dynamic sources which, with the id, comprise a single energy system. One of these he called the ego and the other the superego. The ego seeks to order animal energy by the foresightful calculations of utility and reason—it aims at adjustment to the causal order (which Freud regularly calls "reality"). The superego represents the self-concern for acculturation; it seeks to tame the basic libidinal drives by imposing the taboos and sanctions of society, as these have been introjected into the self from the parents and surrogates of society. The superego is felt as "self," and yet it is actually the inward registry of external and arbitrary authority.[23] The whole self is the precarious resultant of these three nonparallel forces; it is the system of desire organized by controls which are partly authoritarian and partly rational. There is a fixed quantum of biological energy and the self is an organized episode of it, in the ongoing process of nature and society.

Harry Stack Sullivan interprets the emergence and structuring of the self in rather different terms. He begins with what he believes are "the two great motors of human behavior and thought." They are "the pursuit of satisfactions and the maintenance of security."[24] By "satisfactions" he refers to the meeting of the primary biological needs: food, drink, sex, sleep and herd contact! Our driving to secure these satisfactions involves the tonic changes in our unstriped musculature; the quest for "pleasure" has an irreducible "physiological substrate." "Throughout life the pursuit of satisfactions is physiologically provoked by increased tone in some unstriped muscles; and the securing of the satisfactions is a decrease of this tone. . . ."[25]

The other aspect of the self-system is more uniquely hu-

man, for it is distinctively social. It is the very deeply motivated desire for acceptance, belonging, approval and the
fear of disapproval, rejection and loss of support. "Security"
is affected by changes in the personal environment and by
the impact of society. The human organism, especially, cannot survive uncared for by society. Disapproval is the sign
of the threat of abandonment; approval the sign of continued support and thus security! Whereas all the physical satisfactions involved the *decrease* in tonus of the autonomic
nervous system, the feeling of security is associated with the
maintenance of tonus in the voluntary (or cerebrospinal)
system.

This double enterprise—satisfaction and security—governs the process in which the self (or "self-system," or "self-
dynamism," to use Sullivan's synonyms)[26] emerges and
finds its individual form. The most crucial aspect of the
process is the perception of and reaction to the *attitudes* of
other persons. Indeed, Sullivan can say, in unacknowledged
agreement with G. H. Mead, that "the self is made up out
of reflected appraisals . . . ; if the self-dynamism is made
up of experience which is chiefly derogatory, then the self-
dynamism will itself be chiefly derogatory."[27] The self-system's relation to others is determined by the way it has assimilated the attitude and action of others. The degrees of
psychopathology reflect the measure of the distortion (or
"parataxis") in the subject's feelings in response to what he
takes to be the estimate of the persons on whom he supposes he must depend. The pattern of the self-system, constructed thus out of appraisal and reaction, builds slowly

and tends to persist tenaciously thereafter. It supplies the cues for future reactions to persons hitherto unknown. Men may react to women in terms of the residue of their para-taxic relations to mothers or sisters—and this distorts the present person-to-person relation because of the uncon-scious influence of memories and attitudes no longer rele-vant.

Thus, for a "cultural analyst" like Sullivan,[28] the human self is the registry of the felt dispositions of significant per-sons; it is the organizing center of the energies of the organ-ism as these are directed toward "satisfactions" and "secu-rity." It is the sum of reflected appraisals—but it is also, in a curious way, an *appraiser* of these appraisals! The self is shaped in the social matrix; it is, indeed, an episode in the social process.

It would be an impertinence for me to offer a critical judgment on the clinical merits of the Freudian and Sulli-vanesque descriptions of the motive forces in the human organism and their patterning. But it is a proper part of our task to take note of their implications which reach beyond the clinic and contribute to our general understanding of this problem of the self. And, from the first, we see that the traditional lines of the body-mind problem have been al-tered past recognition—and this, we might well agree, is a good thing for all concerned. The psychotherapists have shown, without significant disagreement, that whatever else or more the self may be, it is radically rooted in the biologi-cal process; that the interaction of "psyche" and "soma" is not the sign of a duality but of a complex unity. Secondly, these psychotherapeutic explorations into the self have amply confirmed the thesis that selves depend on other selves for the basic shape of selfhood. Self-appraisal and self-development are closely tied to the process of being known and appraised as a self by others. Thus the quality of the personal environment is decisive for the quality of the self. The self is never self-sufficing, and could never emerge alone and independent of society. The gravest threat to selfhood is isolation.[29] Perhaps the most prolific source of the widespread phenomenon of anxiety and guilt is the fear of rejection and irrevocable loneliness. Human selves grow by being known and loved; in an atmosphere of inattention or denigration, they grow defectively and fail of maturation.

The psychotherapists have, then, shown us how fully and integrally involved the self-system is in *every* level of existence, from glands and striped muscles to the highest reach of mind and spirit. This understanding is of immense importance and must be made to apply in every aspect of our interpretation. But they leave us still with our basic question unanswered. Why do *human* selves emerge as they do —and with such extraordinary characteristics—in a process which is so nearly similar for many other "irritable organisms" which nevertheless develop so differently. Other organisms have hedonic drives, they are conditioned by their congeners, they seek satisfactions and securities, exhibit "mental topographies" not unlike Freud's triune-self of id, ego and superego—and develop energy systems which are impressively integrative, biologically stable and efficient. The human self emerges in a matrix which has very much in common with that in which simian "selves" emerge; the human fetus and infant show plainly their close kinship with their primate cousins—and the human adult does not disengage himself from the animal kingdom. But the human self appears to vary more widely from simian selves than the differences in their genetic processes would seem to allow. And *human* selves seem to be affected by *human* appraisals in a fashion quite distinct from the appraisals of other "selves" in their environment. Inter*personal* relations appear to be quite different from inter*simian*. Thus, we have two questions: Are these alleged differences apparent or real—and can either answer be established *empirically?* If apparent—*why* the appearance; if real, why the actual difference? The reductionist doctrine of the self must show empirically that the differences between human selves and other selves are natural developments in an evolutionary continuum; that "mind" and "spirit" and "personality" are symmetrical extensions of the organic process—and nothing more! Then, but not till then, can they invoke the law of parsimony to foreclose on the doctrine of the substantial self.

Unless we have begged this question at the outset, from either side, we are here before one of the most elusive and endlessly interesting aspects of man's inquiry about himself. One of the wisest analyses of the problem I know is to be found in Sir Charles Sherrington's Gifford Lectures of 1937–38. Sherrington was one of the most eminent of modern physiologists, and a psychologist of stature. There is a summary section which deserves extended quotation, for it defines our problem, in different terms, and suggests the essential premise for our answer:[30]

Not so long ago expectation was entertained by many that mind would with the growth of knowledge prove to be energy of some form, as yet perhaps not delimited. . . . This expectation has not been fulfilled. Further knowledge has not brought the two together. It has more definitely parted them. . . . Today there is a tendency to stress "mind" as dynamic. As metaphor this may be admirable. But it is prone to suggest that mind is "energy."

Mind, for anything perception can compass, goes therefore in our spatial world more ghostly than a ghost. Invisible, intangible, it is a thing not even of outline; it is not a "thing." It remains without sensual confirmation, and remains without it for ever. Stripped to nakedness there remains to it but itself. What then does that amount to? All that counts in life. Desire, zest, truth, love, knowledge, "values," and, seeking metaphor to eke out expression, hell's depth and heaven's utmost height. Naked mind. We live at a moment hitherto unmatched, for our planet has just evolved mind in us to the pitch that we can take in our local situation of this present as we walk her side. Mind, yoked with life, how varied in its reaction! It will sit down and watch life acquiescent, or on the other hand take life and squeeze it like an orange.

And that other concept, energy; what of its yield? We saw that Time has winnowed its harvest too. How much remains? The perceptible world. All that the space-time continuum contains; gathered harmoniously into one category, a category which nothing which does not act on sense can enter and which all that does so act does enter. It sets us wondering whether what we sense can be just purely outcome of our mind. If so, it seems strange it should fall into so sharply different a category from all the other products of the mind. With this hint implicit in it, the perceived world is then our other concept's fruit.

Between these two, naked mind and the perceived world, is there then nothing in common? Together they make up the sum total for us; they are all we have. We called them disparate and incommensurable. Are they then absolutely apart? Can they in no wise be linked together? They have this in common—we have already recognized it—they are both concepts; they both of them are parts of knowledge of one mind. They are thus therefore distinguished, but are not sundered. Nature in evolving us makes them two parts of the knowledge of one mind and that one mind our own. We are the tie between them. Perhaps we exist for that.

The human self is an integer of mind and energy—and of more, perhaps—but the elements integrated in the self-system are not interconvertible. Mind and spirit have emerged in an energic process and cannot be reduced to it without ruthless excision of significant data. And this, I suggest, is what every purely empirical analysis of this problem does and is bound to do!

It is worth noting that even in their denials of the transcendental reality of the self, the psychotherapists cannot avoid relating it to ultimates beyond it. For Freud, the id is not only more primitive than superego or ego; there is an interesting sense in which it operates as a transcendental unity of afference.

The processes of the system Ucs (unconscious system) are timeless; i.e. they are not ordered temporally, are not altered by the passage of time, in fact bear no relation to time at all.

The time-relation also is bound up with the work of the system Cs (conscious system).

The processes of the Ucs (unconscious system) are just as little related to reality.[31]

"Reality" here, as typically in Freud, refers to the causal order of the empirical world. It is true that Freud threw his own full commitment on the side of the ego—reason and object-love. "Where id was, there let ego be"—was a short form of the Freudian gospel. But his biologistic premise forced him to a dim view of the human prospect. At bottom and in the end, the human self is a complex energy system striving inordinately for the inappropriate. It is no wonder that religion was, for Freud, an illusion which nurtures false hopes of what man should expect from life.

The cultural analysts have greatly exceeded the orthodox Freudian concept of the self by emphasizing its societal and interpersonal relations. Whereas Freud was chiefly impressed by the inhibitive role of culture, Horney, Sullivan, Fromm and their colleagues have seen and explored the positive and normative role of culture for the making of personality. But they have, in fact, succeeded only in pushing our essential question one step further toward a real transcendence of the human self. The individual self, they say, is the sum of its reflected appraisals from significant other selves. These appraisers would also, presumably, be respective sums of appraisal—and so on and on. And if this be the case, what then is society? Is it a vast and incredibly complex equilibrium of individual reactor systems, each contingent on a vector within the whole and the whole contingent upon the harmony of the integrative action of the respective individual entities? This is an interesting notion indeed, but full of unresolved difficulties. Society is certainly the matrix of selfhood and the medium of all self-activity. But is it the self's creator, sustainer and redeemer? This would seem to follow from the thesis that the self is *nothing but* the sum of personal appraisal. But what of human society—has it a ground, an end, a reference beyond itself? Is its model to be found in nature? Society is a false ultimate. It is the matrix but not the source of selfhood!

The Christian is bound, by the radical implications of his faith, to maintain the conviction that the human self is singular, substantial, responsible—and not subsumed within the species, nor yet within nature and society. Man exists as an item in nature but his distinctively human existence comes from his *self-participation* in an order and a purpose which transcends nature. All the various ways in which the human self transcends the empirical systems in which the naturalist would place him point to an ultimate reference: the human self is a deliberate and unique creature of God. Out of love, God has designed a community of finite creatures endowed with the capacities of response to, reliance on, Himself in love and blessedness. Each such creature would be, therefore, singular, perdurable and free, a project of God's will to build up and rectify a community covenanted to Him in faithfulness, rationality and love. It is the reality of God which guarantees the reality of the human person; it is the love of God which defines the person's highest hope and good; it is God's self-disclosure in Christ

and immanent presence in the Holy Spirit which creates
the atmosphere in which we can truly know ourselves as all
along we have been known[32] and accept ourselves as we
have been accepted in His grace. The human self emerges
in the dynamic patterns of nature and society, but the intention behind and within that emergence is a special project of God, who has made us for Himself—and made us to
be ourselves!

The human self is an *object*, of a sort—and, as such, can
be described as the empiricists have described us. The self
as an object is a system of energies (or, more precisely, a
system of several systems of energy). In a healthy and mature person, these energies are organized into a pattern
characterized by identity (self-sameness), continuity and
responsible freedom. These are the *signs* of the person—
and the measure of his maturity. They are summed up in a
word used more often than there is psychological warrant
for it: *integrity*. Both the energies thus organized and the
patterns of organization are being most usefully illuminated by the theories and practice of psychotherapy. Man,
as *object*, is indeed the proper study of—the sciences of
man!

But the human self is also, and more essentially, a *subject*, which never appears to the view of others or even to
the most determined introspection. There is *something* beyond the self as object which corresponds to Kant's "transcendental unity of apperception;" *something* which is pre-
supposed in all self-appearance and self-activity; *something*
which "personalizes" the human organism's responses to its

environment. It is the "I" to another's "Thou." It is the prius of will and action, of freedom and responsibility. This self-subject transcends the causal order without abrogating it. It is this *subject*-self which is related to God—and always as to divine Subject, never as to *a* divine Object. The human self is finite and, as *object*, it touches all other finites whatsoever, in some sort of relation; either of knowledge or efference. But the self as *subject* touches the infinite; it is the meeting place of time and eternity, of man and God. Thus the self escapes itself, in freedom, and is, therefore, never a fully predictable or manipulable object. But the self returns to itself and shares, in reason and process, in all the events of its existence. The object-self is in the world and of the world (hence, it falls within the provinces of the sciences). The subject-self is in the world but of the world. And yet these are not two separated selves, nor even halves of one self. The human self is an integer, but a complex integer of "two natures"!

Man as object of investigation and man as freedom are known to us from radically different sources. The former is a content of knowledge, the latter a fundamental trait of our faith. But if freedom for its part becomes a content of knowledge and an object of investigation, a special form of superstition arises:

Faith stands on the road to freedom that is not an absolute and not an empty freedom, but that is experienced as the possibility of being given or not given to oneself. It is only through freedom that I become certain of transcendence. By freedom, to be sure, I attain to a point of independence from the world, but precisely through the consciousness of my radical attachment to transcendence. For it is not through myself that I am.

Superstition on the other hand arises by way of a some- thing that is the express content of faith, and thus also through a supposed knowledge of freedom. A modern form of superstition for example is psychoanalysis taken as a phi- losophy, and the pseudo-medicine that makes man's freedom a supposed object of scientific research.

As I conceive of the nature of my humanity, so I conceive of transcendence—i.e. I conceive of it either as something that limits me or as something that enables me to soar, it is superstition steeped in the object (hence associated with scientific aberration), or faith, inner experience of the Com- prehensive (hence associated with the consummation of non- knowledge).

Man, in common with everything he sees around him, in common with the beasts, is branded as a finite creature. But his human finiteness *cannot become self-contained,* in the same sense as the animal.

Every animal is perfect in its own way, in its limitation it fulfils itself within a continually repeated life cycle. It is ex- posed only to the natural process in which all things merge and are brought forth. Only man cannot fulfil himself in his finiteness. It is only man whose finiteness involves him in his- tory, in which he strives to realize his potentialities. His openness is a sign of his freedom.[33]

The self needs must be explained in its finiteness, but all such explanations must have an open end to the mystery of the self as it responds to the infinite. God comes to man, knows him in his total existence, makes Himself known to man in the offer of love and the demand for righteousness. In this process, God draws man beyond his purely "natural" share in the causal order and *thrusts* him into freedom. The human organism becomes an authentic *person,* then, not merely through the impulsions of nature and society described in the psychodynamic account of human growth —but also by the impulsion and purpose of the Creator-Spirit, ground and sustaining power of existence.

If this, or something like it, is the gist of the Christian notion of the self, it is easy to see how the reductionist view of the self, prevalent in psychotherapeutic doctrine, stands in conflict—the conflict of opposing *faiths.* The notion of the self as an emergent of nature, dismisses the idea of God as superfluous—one may wonder a bit if this is not an unconscious intent of the doctrine. A great celebrant of natural vitality, Nietzsche, felt obliged to get rid of God, for "only when there is no God does man become free."[34]

If the self is merely a node in a complex causal series, the whole question of transcendence and man's relation to God becomes irrelevant. If self-activity is energized and structured by the sovereign needs of "satisfactions" and "security" (hedonism) then the idea of an "I-Thou" encounter between God and man is pious illusion. If the self is a system of fully-ordered stimulus-response patterns, then the problems of meaning and value, of freedom and blessedness are soluble, theoretically, on a wholly secularist basis. The self produced by nature and society becomes a self apart from God, a self with no need of God—and God becomes a human projection, fit only for the feeble and the credulous. Man becomes man in *this* world, man for himself, man the master of his "soul." Self-realization, for such a man, must be conceived and accomplished within the limits of the vitality and the order of nature, taken as the sum and ground of all existence. The human person, so conceived, will have existential concerns and moral values which will be expressed in serious commitment—but the commitment will produce a religion of humanity, an order of aspiration and hope wholly contained within whatever is taken to be the round of nature.

For the Christian, this view of man fails, not in the middle distance, but in its narrow field of final vision which obscures the primordial and ultimate relation of man to God. It disposes of the issue of self-transcendence by denying that such an issue is significant. It disclaims metaphysical inquiry, but it does manage to *imply* very far-reaching metaphysical assertions and denials. Such a view, incorporated into the psychotherapeutic enterprise, proves useful in interpreting man's distortion of his freedom and rationality, both in neurosis and in the rigid-normal compromise. But it fails to account for the unique and elusive mystery of the self in freedom and religious devotion—and turns failure into triumph by declaring that there is no mystery.[35]

The Christian view of man begins with man's radical finitude and dependence and drives through the levels of nature and society to ground existence in the divine creativity of God. Man is God's creature, known, beloved, "respected." In our human existence there is a double order of apprehending which operates in every crucial situation of crisis and choice. There is our comprehension of *causality* and there is our apprehension of *destiny*. Finite events and quantifiable objects are known in their interaction according to laws or exact generalizations. In this order, we know by possessing, by controlling or prediction. Persons are involved in the causal order, not only as observers and recorders, but also as *objects*, acted upon and acting in determinate fashion—and this comprises the vast bulk of ordinary and "common-sense" experience.

On the other hand, our apprehension of destiny is a *different kind* of noetic encounter, although it is an integral part of the same person who is also and at the same time involved in the causal order. At this deeper level, we know by being possessed, by being known and "respected" by the reality which is ground and support of our having and our being. Obviously, our noetic apparatus is finite. This limits the operation and outreach of empirical inquiry. The empirical world is a common one—the possibility of science rests on the universality and unanimity of scientific truth—but our common world points beyond itself to a real world which transcends our positive knowledge but not the outreach of our thought and faith. And it is from this real world that the stimuli to freedom and responsibility—selfhood and our destiny—come, to be mixed into the empirical enterprises in which we are engaged.[36]

It is quite clear by now that an essential part of the Christian notion of the person is responsible freedom—the will is the center of the human self. The psychotherapists, whether mechanist or humanist in their naturalism, have the problem of will and freedom on their hands as well. It is interesting, however, to see how much discussion of personality there is which never focuses this question sharply nor explores it past the surface. From among the exceptions to this general evasion, we may note two explicit statements which profess to speak representatively. One is an article by Robert P. Knight,[37] a neo-Freudian; the other by Patrick Mullahy,[38] a Sullivanite. Despite their difference in psychotherapeutic theory, they are surprisingly close together in their view of "freedom." Knight assumes, correctly, that "determinism is a fundamental tenet of all science." He supposes that this precludes any sort of "indeterminism" in human behavior—this would be beyond the reach of science! Human freedom is the *subjective feeling* which accompanies successful adjustment to the strictly determinate causal nexus which governs our actions. Man is free when he is in harmony with and consciously acting in the causal process—without compulsion or anxiety and with the sense of well-being in this co-operation with the inevitable. Unfreedom is the anxiety, frustration and estrangement we feel when we are maladjusted to the conditioning forces at play upon us—and this is a prolific source of crippling bondage in the neurotic. The aim of therapy is to create or enhance the feeling of "freedom," of harmony and co-operation in the natural ordering of life—and this is the mark of the mature person! Psychotherapy is a highly successful aid in transforming compulsion into freedom.

Mullahy is sure that

> willing and its efficacy is just as much a matter of observation as is anything else. It occurs under determinate conditions. But it is the whole person who wills, a person who has

> mental, emotional and sensuous aspects, not a machine-like
> organism which acts blindly according to the way it is con-
> ditioned, or impelled by inward machinery.
>
>   . . . To be free is to be able to act in accordance with the
> powers that one possesses under the conditions of human
> life. . . . In other words, man is free when he is determined
> by the requirements and conditions of his own nature; and
> only when he expresses his nature can values and ideals have
> genuine authority and appeal.[39]

But, in the perspective of "critical naturalism," which Mullahy professes, what are the conditions of our human nature? Do they include self-transcendence? The answer
would appear to be "No," and thus we are back again in
what William James used to call "a soft determinism."

There are admirable motives for maintaining this general
view—all except the final contention that this outlook is
self-sufficient. One of the good motives is to deny the antithesis of *indeterminism,* and to affirm that human events
belong to an orderly and intelligible process. Another valid
motive is to deny that human willing could, under any circumstance, affect an increase in the fixed quantum of the
world's energy system—and also to affirm that all human
actions operate in the same energy system as do all other determinate events. One may readily agree to all this and still
be far from being persuaded that determinism—even a *soft*
determinism—gives us an account of the experience of *responsibility* which we know as an essential aspect of selfhood. And the layman might even wonder at the therapeutic utility of a concept of freedom which considers it a
subjective feeling or one which defines it in terms of "the

requirements and conditions of one's own nature." As for the first, the subjective feeling would signify an illusion, which would have to be masked from the unfree patient, or else maintained as a useful fiction. And, for the second, who knows, exactly or exhaustively, just what the requirements and conditions of our human nature actually are? Who, indeed, but God—who has been classified as "unemployable" by the naturalist?

Christian reflection about the self and its freedom has produced widely various doctrines, but it has always been based on two basic premises drawn from the biblical witness to God's dealings with men. The first is that the will is the deepest and strongest bond of the *unity* of the self. It is in the *decisions* which man makes for or against God's offer of love and God's demands for righteousness, that he grows into unity or falls into disunity. Man is a responsive and responsible creature. To respond to God in faithfulness is responsibility. To respond in unfaithfulness is the essence of irresponsibility. Similarly, men are faithful or unfaithful in their response to others. We do not merely *reflect* the appraisals of others. We ourselves *make* appraisals and decisions, and the process is always more than reflex action. Finally, in our inner personal existence, the decisions we make of self-rejection or self-acceptance turn on acts of choice in which we are—or may be—aware of our responsibility or irresponsibility. Throughout the Bible, in a hundred different ways, we recognize the common theme that God never treats man as a puppet but always "respects" him as a responsible person. Thus He deals in love and pa-

tience and judgment and mercy with men who are meant
to be free and whose freedom-to-be-responsible is never
taken away nor ridden down, even when their sin and irresponsibility bring tragedy and woe in their train.

The second biblical theme concerning man's freedom is
that finiteness and freedom co-exist in the unity of the self
and its system of behavior. Nowhere, in Christian thought,
is the power of free will understood as a power to free man
from God or to make man infinite, or to remove man from
his radical involvement in the causal order of nature. But
the biblical view does make it plain that natural causality
never exhausts the matter of man's freedom and destiny.
Freedom exists in finiteness; man is the creature whose finiteness thrusts him into freedom. For man, freedom is the
mode by which he responds to the infinite, and it is indeed
the willing of the whole person, with all the powers of his
nature, in interaction with God who is the Creator of "the
requirements and conditions of our nature" including our
freedom.

The Christian would find it useful to explore the general
thesis of the duplex order of "causality" in human reaction.
There is natural causality and there is will causality and the
two co-exist, not as rivals, but as complications of the process of human motivation and decision.

By this freedom the will of a rational being, as belonging to
the sensuous world, recognizes itself to be, like all other efficient causes, necessarily subject to the laws of causality,
while in practical matters, in its other aspect as a being in

itself, it is conscious of its existence as determinable in an intelligible order of things.[40]

Human action is both determinate in nature and determinable by the self! Will causality is the *power to intend a significant project or end which is immanent and optative.* It is the power of an *agent*, or actor—not an automaton. Once *intended* by the will, the project's realization enters into and is determined by the conditions of physical causality in the situation. "The potency of the will, therefore, is defined (i) by the occurrence of such projects in situations of choice and (ii) by the capacities of our psychological organism in given circumstances."[41] In any experience of "moral struggle" we may discern the preconditioning factors which shape the possibilities of choice, but we may also, as I believe with Farrer, be aware of a nondetermined, uniquely human act, as truly present as the natural processes, which are so much more directly observable.

> What we are looking for is the element of sheer will, and this we have found to lie in a mysterious intending of the project supposed by us to be the right one, an intending not determined by anything, but which simply actualises or does not actualise itself and, therewith, the process of the project.[42]

Every human act, involving crisis and deliberation, may be understood from two standpoints, both of them relevant to an understanding of the act and the actor. If we consider a past act or a probable future one, we may analyze it as determinate, with the self as an *object* acted upon by the conditioning forces we are able to observe. Our conclusion, in such a perspective, is that the outcome was or will be determined by the combination of causal factors present. The option chosen is the most strongly motivated among the possible options. This is to be inferred from the fact of its having been chosen. But was there anything free or generative here, or only an acquiescence in necessity? *After* a decision, it is possible to infer that, taking everything into account that went into the decision, it had to happen as it did. But this begs our real question—and assumes that natural causality is *all* there is to a human act. But what makes an actually chosen option the strongest among many? If, then, we consider our experience in a *present* crisis, we are aware of a significant dimension not observable in past or future acts.[43] There is the consciousness of immediate agency and responsibility, a power to intend, to desire, to initiate the "will," to commit ourselves over and beyond the pressures of necessity. Every man knows moments of deliberation, when spontaneous action is blocked, in which he finds himself reviewing the multiple possibilities, *intending* one and thereby removing the others as possibilities for *that* time. Such acts of will may be in harmony with reason and with the felt imperatives of the divine will. Or, they may be irrational or unfaithful. But they will be human—the most distinctive and uniquely human acts we know or perform. Anything less than this is, in some degree, less than human. The measure of our humanity is our responsibility and the measure of our responsibility is our freedom.

The Christian message could well afford to abandon

many of the aspects of the traditional picture of the human
"psyche"—and the faculty psychology derived from it. It
could greatly profit from the newer psychological insights
into the self's emergence in nature and society. It could go
far in accepting the phenomenological descriptions of the
self provided by the various schools of psychotherapy. But
it must reject any and all *reductions* of selfhood to biological or societal energy systems. And it must insist upon the
uniqueness, freedom and transcendence of the self—a finite
spirit in spiritual relation to infinite Spirit.

The Christian view of man needs to appropriate the
psychotherapeutic ideal of *psychological* autonomy—that is,
man's self-direction undistorted by superego tyrannies and
the arbitrary interventions of other persons. But it also
needs to distinguish autonomy at *this* level from the secularistic conceptions of autonomy in which man is measure
and master of existence as well. The Christian message
makes it plain that man is God's creature; it is from God
that the font of man's being and goodness flows. Our destiny stands in our knowledge of Him and in His service are
our freedom and finiteness perfected.

The importance of this issue between psychotherapy and
Christian thought lies in the implications of the respective
answers for interpersonal relations. The prerequisite for a
productive relation to people is respect and love—which
presuppose, in turn, an estimate of the human person, his
quandaries and his possibilities. What we are able to do for
another person depends, at least in part, on what sort of
being he is—and we ourselves are. This is crucial for psy-

chotherapy because, more than any other of the healing arts, it effects its results through interpersonal relations. The surgeon, and to a lesser degree the physician, achieve their results through measures which a medieval schoolman might have described as *ex opere operato*. Psychotherapy, for all its need for auxiliary medical and surgical techniques —and constant medical supervision and reference—is essentially a personal enterprise and all its significant results are to be measured by qualitative effects in the persons involved. This is why the personal attitudes of patient toward therapist are so important, and why their handling is so decisive in treatment. This is why self-knowledge, self-acceptance and self-affirmation are basic aims in every type of therapy and counseling.

But what about the therapist's or the counselor's estimate of the person before him—and of himself? Our doctrine of the self is bound to affect our interpretation of every interpersonal relation. It will shape the process of our observations and it will suggest the interpretation of the data we collect. If the therapist believes that his patient—and that he himself—are *nothing but* energy systems in a natural process which is itself the only ultimate there is, what then will be his estimate of the goals and ends of therapy? How will he interpret the quandaries men fall into? What will he believe about the possibilities before this man—or any man? And how will he conceive the good ordering of the best life for man? If, alternatively, he works from the inner conviction of his own creatureliness and of God's loving concern for the well-doing and blessedness of His beloved children; if he believes that men are finite yet not fettered by the bonds of finitude—what then will he see and how will he answer the essential questions? Actually, of course, the clinical course of therapy might begin and go forward in its early stages in much the same way—for any given system of therapy—but both the quality and the aims would be discernibly different. And as treatment progressed and as growing psychic health brought up the possibility of searching questions about the self and its ground, the two different sets of assumption would more and more generate two different frames of reference, not only for the termination of therapy but for the succeeding enterprise of living-beyond-therapy.

Christianity's concern for the health of the whole man and psychotherapy's goal of sane, productive living agree in many important ways. If men are to live well, they must know themselves as they are and as they may be. They must be willingly oriented to reality—and rational enough to reject fantasy and wishful thinking as the shaping forces of their hopes and choices. Psychotherapy, as a strictly empirical discipline, cannot tell us what we are—and ought not to tell us we are *nothing but*. Neither can it supply a rigorous description of existence as a whole—although within its limits as an empirical science, its methodology is valid enough. The sciences—and even the practical arts—construct world views derived from basic faith. But they need not suppose that their world views are past changing or that they possess the scientific authority which their empirical constructions may have.

Modern psychotherapy grew up with a world view which, from the Christian standpoint, needs changing and which could very well be changed without sacrificing the validity and usefulness of psychotherapy's practical wisdom. There are no theoretical obstacles in the way of the exploration— by the psychotherapists for themselves—of alternate approaches to an ampler world view than the now archaic "heavenly city of the eighteenth-century philosophers."

It is past time that Dr. Putnam's concerns about the self and the good life should be acknowledged as important by the psychotherapists. It is a good time for them to review and reconstruct the premises within which they conceive and develop their enterprise. If they were willing so to do, they would discover in the Christian perspective an unsuspected treasure of insight into these problems of our human nature, our existence and our destiny.

CHAPTER THREE

The Human Quandary

No one has ever denied that men find life a quandary, replete with perplexities and obscurities in respect of both their existence and their destiny. It is not merely that life sets us problems to solve, stresses to endure, and goals to achieve—and all this in order to produce a maturer, richer self in the successful mastery of these challenges. It is, more deeply, the grim and widely attested human experience of *nonfulfillment*, in life and selfhood. Men come to failures in their lives, sometimes spectacular and appalling failures, sometimes drab and bleak failures, sometimes the subtle failure of rigid-normal "success" in life which masks the inner reality of nonfulfillment. The human quandary is the primary plot or motif of all great literature and art. "Paradise lost" is the pivot of all believable character analysis or construction in drama, opera, novel or poem. "Paradise regained" is the vision of the artist's striving, but always beyond the power of full concreteness. Is this accidental, that none of the world's great *aesthetic* creations concerns a life exempt from the human quandary or unaware of it? The essential meaning of "plot," in literature, is a complication of human affairs in which fulfillment and nonfulfillment are the point-counterpoint of significant action.

There is something dreadfully familiar about the human quandary. Each of us knows it, in his own insight into the discrepancy between the possibility and the actuality of his own life—and those of others about him. H. S. Sullivan hits close home with his grim dictum "that for a great majority of our people . . . the stresses of life distort them to inferior caricatures of what they might have been."[1] Is not the quandary of nonfulfillment a grim familiar of us all?

But there is also something strange—indeed, uncanny—about this aspect of our lives. It ought not to be. It does not fit. It is not a right and harmonious aspect of being—even if we can come to terms with it and so achieve some "peace of mind." There is no *intelligible reason,* inherent in the human situation, why a person, capable of personhood, should not achieve and enjoy the fulfillment of his major ends. No sense at all can be made of the notion that nonfulfillment is a necessary and irremediable state of affairs. It is *wrong* that life should be distorted or frustrated from its positive intent and meaning—and by this we do not mean merely that it is undesirable or inconvenient. Life exhibits actual disvalue, a privation of whatever right and good we acknowledge as the moral pattern of existence. The human quandary is an alien intruder—and thus there has been the agelong temptation to explain it by discovering an external cause or agent as responsible for it. It is a standing, tragic puzzle—and thus the age-old quest for its resolution and redemption.

The human quandary then is both familiar and strange and so calls for an accounting. In the rest of that vast order of animate nature, we find nothing quite like it. Pain and suffering there are in plenty, and the prodigal squandering of teeming life. But there is nothing we can see that resembles such a radical distortion of ends or an awareness of nonfulfillment.

A robust romantic like Walt Whitman could envy the animals,[2]

> They do not sweat and whine about their condition
> They do not lie awake in the dark and weep for their sins,
> They do not make me sick discussing their duty to God. . . .

Yet even his own best poetry came out of his acute sensitivity to the miscarriage of human possibilities. The human quandary requires an accounting that leads beyond, or behind, its description of its symptoms, or the infinite variety of its manifestations. The accounting will, at the last, involve a man's faith, his beliefs about what life is and ought to be, whence it comes and to what end it is intended, and by whom. For the mutilation of life must be measured by the wholeness of life—and we who are not whole ourselves cannot know the meaning of true wholeness within the orbit of our present incompleteness.

Psychotherapy, both as ancient art and modern science, has always been deeply motivated by a concern for men in their quandaries. It has provided us with a series of descriptions of the myriad ways in which men come to grief. It has produced a round of theories to explain the etiology of neurosis and it has developed various clinical techniques for cure or amelioration. But the psychotherapists have not stopped with description and therapy—for man can never be a mere spectator of his fellows, not even "a participant observer." They have had to follow their clinical theories back into their presuppositions, and forward toward some very earnest and far-reaching prescriptions for the moral and social well-being of man. Thus, they offer us an accounting for the human quandary, albeit more implicit than avowed.

The basic conception in their accounting is the human organism's capacity for *growth* and its nisus toward health. "Personality tends towards the state that we call mental health . . . handicaps by way of acculturation notwithstanding. The basic direction of the organism is forward."[3] The aim and pattern of this forward motion is maturation, understood as fulfillment at every level of the organism's capacities. Men are born to grow up, to develop, to become mature and productive persons, capable of object-love and rational management of their lives, without phobias and anxieties, without regressions and illusions. But at least "the great majority" do not make it. Their career lines stop short of the goal, skew off the right path, fail of fulfillment. Why?

Psychotherapy rightly makes a great deal of the extraordinary plasticity of the early years of human life and emphasizes the significance of the longer time span that humans have between birth and maturity. The human animal has far fewer instinctual predeterminations of behavior than any other. This involves the infant and child in a longer and more complicated pattern of dependence on other persons for both his physical "satisfactions" and his emotional "securities." It means that both emotional and intellectual patterns of interpersonal relations are built slowly but in great strength. The patterns thus developed are more decisive for both the shape and rate of growth than any other influences. Everything except the bare potency of personhood has to be achieved in an interpersonal situation which is unstable at best and disastrous at worst. All the various theories stress the precarious journey through the phases that run from birth to maturity, against initial odds and through successive crises which seem to require in advance something of the maturity which will be gained if the crisis is successfully negotiated.

One gets a picture of a tightrope on which the growing person wobbles, unsteady enough inside and threatened by jerks and blunders from those around him. No wonder he falls off. The achievement of human maturity is as difficult to come to as it is impressive when the effort does succeed. There are more possibilities of aberration because there are so many different factors to be integrated at a given time and developed through a time-self continuum. It does not readily occur to psychotherapists to quote Scripture (except the few who do so for their own purposes) but they do manage to furnish extended commentary on Matt. 7:13-14: "The gate is wide and the way is easy, that leads to destruction, and those who enter by it are many. The gate is narrow and the way is hard, that leads to life, and those who find it are few."

Let us ask the psychotherapists how they interpret the processes in which people succeed or fail in finding their paths to maturity. And let us begin with Freud and the Freudians. The simplest proof of Freud's genius is to be found in the fact that, even though many of his own cherished ideas have been rejected by his successors and most of them transcended, in more or less degree, his influence is still inescapable throughout the whole psychotherapeutic movement and, indeed, in modern culture. He had the rare gift of seeing old data in new perspectives and of inspiring faithful disciples to work on new problems finding fresh clues on old trails. He took the results achieved by Charcot and Breuer (his own early co-laborer) with hypnosis, transformed their theories and developed a new practice. A rather shy man, he turned from their preoccupation with hypnosis and suggestion and was led, almost by accident (the sort of accident which never happens to unperceptive people), to the development of his new technique for getting past the blockade of hysterical symptoms. This was *abreaction* (or "free association"). This method of guiding of the patient to speak of anything whatever that occurred to him, without reflection, proved a means of access to "the unconscious mind," which Freud did not discover but of which he was the first great explorer and topographer.[4] Dream interpretation (abreaction at a different level) became a prime auxiliary in psychoanalysis. Freud's most distinctive contribution is just this concept of the access to the unconscious levels of motivation and control with a view to self-discovery, self-recovery and the rational direction of life. In one form or another, this analytic concept has become standard in practically all modern psychotherapy. Out of the data supplied by his explorations into the unconscious, Freud drew a picture of the pattern and form of human development and aberration which still continues, in the main, to be the model of all orthodox Freudians.

Freud and the Freudians came to the conclusion, with Epicurus, Mill and the hedonists generally, that man is motivated, not by conscious ideals and values, but by the primitive twin motives of pleasure and pain. Freud's discoveries led him to believe that the organ systems most directly controlled by the pleasure principle were the alimentary and the genitourinary. These are primitive in the organism's life—and continue basic throughout the total span of human existence.

The first main source of infantile pleasure is feeding, and the primary pleasure zone is the mouth. Thus the Freudians speak of the oral stage of libidinal development.[5] This stage has in it two phases, oral-sucking and oral-biting. The other pole of the alimentary system—evacuation—begins to affect the pattern of development, usually under the stress of the toilet training of the infant. This is the so-called anal (or anal-sadistic) stage of *erotogenous* focalization of pleasure. It also has two phases, one centering on the expulsion, the other the retention of feces. Some Freudians see a *urethral* stage following the anal—but most of them think this is a subphase of the phallic stage, which is, as Freud said, "the forerunner of the final shape of sexual life."[6] It is designed to serve as a bridge between infantile pleasure and the maturity of the genital system and its expression in "object-love" (obviously a very much wider notion than the conventional meanings of "sexuality").

The biological path to maturity runs through these successive stages, each appropriate in its proper time and place but each needing to be superseded by the next—until we come to the mature man, whose biological fulfillment is the basis of social and personal fulfillment as well. But usually there is no smooth passage to maturity. One of the keystones of Freud's theory is the thesis that the growing child forms a libidinal attachment to the parent of the opposite sex. He was sure that this presents the most decisive crisis in a growing person's psychological career. This is the well-known "Oedipal situation." It must be resolved—and the manner of its resolution is the chief determinant of the kind of mental health a person has thereafter.[7]

The latency period is ended by the onset of puberty and the challenge of "mature genitality." The problem of adolescent and adult life is the development and maintenance of appropriate expression of erotic drives—which, for the Freudians, include all the impulses to "social" life as well as "sexual." The problem arises because in any human society the basic hedonic drives cannot find unhindered outlet. It is inherent in the social situation that individuals cannot act just as they please. The pleasure principle is not a sufficient guide for life. There is an order of cause and effect

—which Freud calls "reality"—and the organism must adapt to this or else either die or be crippled. Survival itself requires frustration, but mental health depends on *how* this frustration is organized and directed by the self.

The energic core of the behavioral system is the id. This is the font of drive and desire, spontaneously hedonic, irrational and uneducable. The id, for Freud, is curiously transcendental; it is unaffected by the categories of time, space and causality. It has two main functions: to thrust life forward and then to extinguish it—all this in the unending biological cycle of birth and death.

The ceaseless thrust of the id is patterned, as we have seen, by the rational system of the ego and the arbitrary code of the superego. The superego is no more rational than the id but it does register the effects upon the individual of social approval (and support) and of disapproval (threat of nonsupport). It stands over against the id with the highly moralistic judgment of society—it tries to dam up the surging flow of the id or drive it underground by its powerful weapons of shame, guilt and reprisal. The superego tries to moralize the id—and never succeeds, because its own morality is arbitrary and external. It is the conflict of arbitrary inhibition of arbitrary desire.

> From the point of view of morality, the control and restriction of instinct, it may be said of the id that it is totally nonmoral, of the ego that it strives to be moral, and of the superego that it can be hyper-moral and then becomes as ruthless as only the id can be.[8]

In spite of their fundamental difference, the id and the

super-ego have one thing in common: they both represent the influences of the past (the id the influence of heredity, the super-ego essentially the influence of what is taken over from other people) whereas the ego is principally determined by the individual's own experience . . . !⁹

The ego is that system in the mind which discerns causes and effects and adjusts means to ends, desire to actuality. It is as firmly oriented toward pleasure as the id but it can discriminate between the better and worse ways of erotic satisfaction, since it is concerned with self-preservation and optimal, rather than maximal, enjoyment.

Where people are actually controlled by the taboos of the superego, their behavior will inevitably be immature and potentially neurotic. Man's quandary arises from the clash of these energic systems within himself. The problem is how to fight free of the tyranny of society without falling into a worse predicament. This is why Freud's evangel ("Where id was, there let ego be!") is more hopeful than confident.

An organism so organized (and disorganized) has an unlikely prospect of passing from stage to stage in normal development without serious mishap. Forward progress may be arrested at any one of the erotogenic levels—and wherever this occurs, trouble follows. Frustration generates unpleasure and this, in turn, anxiety; anxiety mobilizes the security-operations of the organism for fight or flight. The disturbance stirs the superego which responds by meting out praise and blame, guilt and self-deprecation. In such a turmoil, the ego gets swamped—squeezed from both sides—

so that behavioral patterns deteriorate, and regress to one or another stage of prematurity. The bulk of human misery stems from the inappropriate resolution of this basic conflict between internal drives which know no law and external codes which have no grace.

Thus, there is an inevitable human quandary, even for men living in the simplest and freest possible social environments. But "civilization" compounds the human predicament and worsens the conflict we have described. In 1927, Freud set down some rather bleak reflections on this problem in a significant little book which he called *Civilization and Its Discontents*. In this essay, he sought to apply the implications of psychoanalytic knowledge to the conflict areas in organized society. Civilized living requires the imposition of curbs and sanctions on the expression of id—impulses. It ranges itself solidly behind the superego and so tends always to thicken the crust of custom. Thus it is that the average man, in the average civilized society, spends most of his energy and intelligence in devising ways to endure the chafings of conventional morality and experimenting with compensatory substitute gratifications. The possibilities of rational sublimations and of mature object-love are seldom glimpsed or realized. And for many of these blind Samsons, religion is a sort of mass psychosis, in which the fiction of the loving heavenly Father holds open the hope that the faithful believer will get a proper reward in heaven for his self-abnegations here below.

Civilization is, then, principally an effort at taming and harnessing human vitality. But the id will not learn to heel or fetch—it cannot be caged or dammed up. Man's aggressive nature cannot be guided by the slender bridle of benevolence and the love of peace. Beneath all masks, there is the thrust of life and there is the instinct to its extinction.[10] These instincts unleash titanic forces, they wreak vast, irrational destruction, wear themselves out in fury. War is a collective outburst of this ineradicable human aggressiveness. In 1932, Albert Einstein wrote Freud to enlist his aid in the cause of peace, "posing the question of what can be done to protect mankind from the curse of war." Freud's reply is uncommonly blunt. He is himself opposed to war —every civilized man is, he says. But "there is no use in trying to get rid of men's aggressive inclinations . . . it is enough to try to divert them to such an extent that they need not find expression in war."[11] The human quandary, for the individual and the group, in this irreducible conflict, which even in the relatively mature is still interminable.[12] The end is wrought for us all by *Thanatos,* which is always ready to care for the stragglers.

This is a grim view of man's lot and the tender-minded will turn away from it in distaste, failing to see the positive and constructive intent which animates Freud's work. It is important to notice the undertones of pathos in Freud's own feelings as he contemplates the import of his doctrines.[13] But there is also a vital courage and a deep care for human good—as he understood the matter. He believed that his empirical evidence forced the conclusions to which he had come and that his views of life and destiny were required by his fidelity to the scientific method.

Freud's account of the human quandary compares favorably, as to bleakness, with any theologian's analysis of the plight of sinful man. The very core of human selfhood—its transcendental unity of afference—is irresponsible and uneducable. The equivalent of this in theological teaching would be to say that God made man to be a sinner—and this, by the way, is a formal and substantial heresy! In the Freudian estimate of existence, it is illusory for man to expect any ideal fulfillment of his highest aspirations (typically, the illusion of religion). Reason may provide a partial mastery over nature and society. Analytic therapy is useful in the reduction of neurotic symptoms and "in replacing insecure repressions by reliable and ego-syntonic controls."[14] But this cannot be thoroughgoing. The best possible prospect is a compromise between unlimited desire and limited satisfaction. Nonfulfillment is the rule of human life. It is the part of wisdom to know this, to understand why it is so and, making the most and the best use of our rational powers, enjoy what life can yield of happiness and content.

The genius of Freud, and his dominant ideas, have continued to guide the main lines along which modern psychotherapy has developed. But, almost from the beginning, new themes and variations began to appear, as extensions, corrections and protests. Adler and Jung very early broke with Freud and went their separate ways. Alfred Adler was impressed by the extent and effect of anxiety in neurotic behavior and connected it, not with sexual frustration, but with the inferiority and insecurity feelings which arise out of the felt weaknesses of the infant and child—especially,

as he thought, the awareness of organ inferiorities.[15] *Power*
is the human problem; sex is a prime symbol and agency in
the power struggle. Human infancy is a state of anxiety-
generating powerlessness, but deep in the infant's motivation is the desire for status and self-directed dominance of
his life situation. The human quandary, for Adler, derives
from the low-probability prospect of an individual's passing
from powerless infancy to powerful maturity without serious psychological mishap. The anxiety bestirred by powerlessness prompts the infant and child into irrational and
inappropriate stratagems of aggression, refuge and compensation. Most of all, he feels himself in *competition* (and
the threat of being outdone or deprived by others). He re-
acts to this with behavior patterns that are too rigid or
stereotyped, overbold or fainthearted—distorted with illusion and unreason. The human plight is that we cannot
accept ourselves as we actually are and our life situations as
they actually are. Thus defeats and frustrations tempt us to
compensatory fictions (fantasies, daydreams, psychosomatic
illness) and these serve as neurotic substitutes, or distrac-
tions for rational action.

Adler saw more clearly than Freud the normative role of
society in providing the matrix of self-emergence and self-
definition. Freud was, primarily, a biologist; he saw the social group chiefly as censor and inhibitor of individual drives
and actions. Adler understood that the group supplies the
positive form of self-development. But he saw this interpersonal relationship largely in the terms of *laissez-faire*
competition and rank. Aggressiveness ("the competitive

ego") is ingredient in human nature as such. Society is the arena of this struggle. The family group provides a rehearsal for the drama to be played out later on a larger stage—and the habits developed there of dealing with stress, threat and frustration tend to shape the individual's psychological character for life.

Good human relations, however, require something better than competition. Men need "a community feeling" and the experience of noninvidious co-operation. In this way, the drives to self-assertion and aggression can be partially sublimated and partially harnessed to a larger good than the individual's self-concern. In Adler's view, sex plays its significant role in this drama of interpersonal adjustment, more often as a means to power and status than as an irrepressible biologic dynamism. In a very interesting way, Adler's psychological theories have much in common with the free-enterprise theories of economics and politics of the late nineteenth century. They assume, on the one hand, that human life is involved in the struggle for "the survival of the fittest" and, on the other, that there is some kind of pre-established moral harmony in which the individual's successful serving of his own interests is actually his best service to society and the general good ("enlightened self-interest"). But the quandary remains. Men is a dependent being, and the society upon which he must depend is a precarious support and an unreliable context for self-fulfillment.

Adler was an optimist—and he had high hopes for the transformation of society by the application of psychological wisdom. But his analysis of the human situation is generally recognized as far less penetrating and realistic than Freud's. Adler's influence in modern psychotherapy has, on the whole, been more indirect than direct. His productive ideas have been taken over and incorporated into more comprehensive and profound systems of psychology.[16]

Carl Gustav Jung began as an ardent Freudian, but after a short term as faithful disciple, he launched out in a different direction and finally broke with Freud altogether. Freud was bitter about Jung's "deviation" and the subsequent history of psychotherapy has been widely affected by the deep antipathy between the two men and their doctrines. Freud attributed Jung's defection as due chiefly to his drawing back from the central Freudian thesis of the primacy of the sexual factor in human life. Jung, for his part, characterized his differences with Freud thus:[17]

The Viennese [Freudian] School takes the standpoint of an exclusive sexualistic conception, while that of the Zurich School [Jungian] is symbolistic. The Viennese School interprets the psychological symbol, semiotically, as a sign or token of certain primitive psychosexual processes. Its method is analytical and causal.

The Zurich School recognizes the scientific feasibility of such a conception but denies its exclusive validity, for it does not interpret the psychological symbol, semiotically only, but also symbolistically, that is, it attributes a positive value to the symbol.

The value [of the symbol] does not depend merely on historical causes; its chief importance lies in the fact that it has a meaning for the actual present and for the future, in their psychological aspects. For to the Zurich School the symbol is not merely a sign of something repressed and concealed, but it is at the same time an attempt to comprehend and to point out the way of the further psychological development of the individual. Thus we add a *prospective* import to the retrospective value of the symbol.

Jung was convinced that there is a sort of primal psychic energy derived from the life process *in toto*; sex is only a part of this and not the most important part, at that.

Jung sought to develop a concept of libido, which is admittedly more speculative than Freud's instinctual theory, and much more complex.[18] From it, we can begin to understand what, for Jung, the human quandary really is. The life processes generate a *surplus* of psychic energy—more than is required to maintain the biological functions of the human organism. The purpose of such a surplus is to provide energy for the acculturation and socialization of the human person, at a level above the animal goals of sex and survival. The patterns by which this libidinal energy is given form and life are typically *symbolic*. The human animal becomes a human person as he participates in the knowledge and use of the *symbols* which enable people to communicate and share experience beyond simple gestures and signs.[19]

Private symbol-making will not do. It is, indeed, the typical mark of aberration and neurosis. Only as our symbols are shared by others are we mutually related. And only as we understand and participate in the universal archetypal symbols can we find valid forms of expression for our surplus psychic force. Every person shares, most often unknowingly, in the inconceivably rich complex of racial memories and experience residues in human history. The individual's consciousness is a relatively narrow focus of this residue and consists chiefly of self-analyzed experience and the rational connections with law, causality and truth which the mind has been able to make. But each of us has "a personal unconscious" which is a sort of reservoir of repressed and forgotten "object-images" (that is, events as we interpreted them at the time, stored in amnestic oblivion). And beyond this is "the *collective* unconscious," still more archaic and diffuse. This is the sum of "the primordial images" or "archetypes" of age-old human experience which we inherit from the human past and from the universal human spirit.[20]

The principal archetypes are, naturally, familial. They center around the images of father, mother and child, *anima* and *animus*—and the symbolic systems which are derived from all of these. The socialization of the individual follows the extension of shared symbols of this sort. The most productive form of universal symbol systems is religion. This is why Jung was so deeply interested in religion and so sure that the greatest need of mankind is to find an adequate religious faith and understanding. There is a familiar quotation in *Modern Man in Search of a Soul*, which highlights this:[21]

Among all my patients in the second half of life—that is to say, over thirty-five—there has not been one whose problem in the last resort was not that of finding a religious outlook on life. It is safe to say that every one of them feel ill because he had lost that which the living religions of every age have given to their followers, and none of them has been really healed who did not regain his religious outlook. This of course has nothing whatever to do with a particular creed or membership of a church.

Trouble comes for a man when he tries to ignore or defy his involvement in this web of universal meaning. Jung's famous typology of extraversion and introversion and his schematism of awareness[22] are interpretive theories which analyze the myriad ways individuals manage or fail in their adjustment to the symbol systems in which they live and move and have their being.

For Jung, therefore, the gist of the human quandary is the aberration which follows upon self-withdrawal, from nonparticipation in the wide community of the human spirit. Isolation, estrangement, alienation—these are the characteristic terms to describe neurosis and human disorder. And, since in the very nature of the case, the human being is poorly prepared to manage privacy and participation, the probabilities of aberration are very high. The human woe we see and feel is not surprising, after all.

Otto Rank stood closer to Freud than to either Adler or Jung, but he broke with orthodox psychoanalysis in his theory of the incidence and meaning of neurosis. He substituted what is, curiously enough, a theory with a concept of an aboriginal paradise and a temporal expulsion from it. The paradise is, of course, the prenatal equilibrium of oceanic peace. Birth is "the fall" and all the rest of life is shaped by the memories of the lost perfection and the yearning to recover it. The birth trauma generates what Rank called "primal anxiety," which continues to affect our feelings and actions throughout the whole of life. The difference between "normal" development and "neurosis" or "psychosis" is the degree to which a person has succeeded or failed in coping with this primal anxiety and its psychic residues.[23]

Primal anxiety begets fear, the fear of separation and non-support. And this, in turn, prompts the individual to surrender his own demand for freedom and selfhood and to depend on others and to find substitute supports. But this renunciation of self-will is crippling; it invites tyranny and neurotic reactions to the tyrannical. The human quandary, in Rank's view, is the loss of freedom and the struggle to regain it. The therapist's task is to free the patient from his fear of freedom. This makes for a much more "active" form of therapy, which Rank called "will therapy."[24]

The psychotherapeutic movement went into a slump in the nineteen-twenties.[25] Practice had outrun theory and was itself losing momentum. The chief impetus in the recovery of a new vitality in doctrine—which in turn affected practice —came from America, and especially among three groups which took their new departures from notions neglected or underdeveloped by the orthodox Freudians. These groups have been notably independent in their inquiries and clinical procedure and have produced some very significant modifications and developments of the European patterns with which they began. As examples for our purposes, we may limit ourselves to Franz Alexander (as a leader among American neo-Freudians), Jules Masserman (as spokesman for the "psychobiologists") and H. S. Sullivan (as the principal system builder among the cultural analysts).

Alexander and his colleagues accept most of the basic Freudian ideas about instinctual motivation, but reject his later death-instinct theory and also his pessimism about the irreformability of the id. Moreover, they have moved to correct Freud's singular myopia about the cultural context of psychogenic illness and his superficial understanding of the psychology of women. In a matter of therapy itself, they have developed new methods of handling the transference situation (the relation between analyst and analysand).[26]

Their account of the human quandary, however, follows the basic Freudian outline. The struggle of the ego to achieve or maintain a rational mastery of the erotic drives and social pressures is an unequal contest. In desperation, the ego resorts to repression, "a primitive device of the ego to maintain its integrity."[27] But repression does not suffice, and disorder reappears. Anxiety arises from the ego's failures, "internalized fear"; this is rooted in attachments to and conflicts with parents and their resolution (Oedipal situation). This anxiety prompts the ego to substitute measures: "reaction-formations," rationalization, displacement, sublimation.[28] The primary difficulty in living stems from the hard fact that our unavoidable desires find unsuitable expression in unmanageable situations. The psychoanalyst verifies anew the bitter plaint of the Lord Chancellor in *Iolanthe*,

Love, unrequited, robs me of my rest.

Psychotherapy may greatly aid the ego in its mastery of its business, but it still must operate within a drastically limited hope of the human possibility. The human plight is both universal and radical. Life's true wisdom lies in a rational compromise between desire and fulfillment. Yet this is not a counsel of defeat or despair. Alexander calls rational and resolute men to what he conceives to be a positive program of productive living.[29]

An American psychiatric development as definitely biologistic as Freud's but quite independent of Freudian orthodoxy may be seen in the pioneer work of Adolf Meyer and the elaboration of his theories by Strecker, Billings and Masserman.

Masserman has formulated, in rather independent fashion, the basic principle of what he calls a "biodynamic theory of behavior." The first of these (the "principle of motivation") indicates the focus and emphasis of this general viewpoint:

> Behavior is basically actuated by the physiologic needs of the organism and is directed towards the satisfaction of those needs.[30]

It is easy to see that, in such a perspective, that there is nothing uniquely human about the human quandary, save

in degree of complication. Our problems in living arise from
the pressures and deprivations of the situation—and our
maladapted or substitutive reactions to it. Man's predicament is to have to seek the best compromise in a situation
which is neither symmetrical nor harmonious for human
existence.[31]

In contrast to biologistic psychotherapy, the cultural analysts have sought to analyze human behavior in its social
and interpersonal matrix. The most creative theorists in this
general group, thus far, are H. S. Sullivan, Karen Horney,
Erich Fromm and Frieda Fromm-Reichmann—and the influence of their work is steadily widening in American psychotherapy, and beyond. There is, of course, important
variety within the movement, but, for our purposes, it is
more significant to observe their essentially common approach to the problems of human growth and fulfillment.
It has an especial interest for the Christian because of the
uncommon stress upon personal and social values in human
life. These analysts begin with the assumption that social,
and not biological, factors are primary in *human* life. Moreover, as they see it, human life is both in essence and
potency, co-operative, communal, interdependent.

Among the cultural analysts, Harry Stack Sullivan is the
most original and thoroughgoing theorist thus far produced
in America. From his remarkable experiences as a clinician,
he undertook to build up a complicated and comprehensive
theory of human growth—which combines a high degree
of psychological sophistication and philosophical naïveté.
Psychiatry, in his conception of it, is simply identical with

the study of man. "The field of psychiatry is the field of interpersonal relations, under any and all circumstances in
which these relations exist."[32] It is interested in persons in
their "integrations" with other persons. But, as we have
seen, he virtually denies the notion of individual personhood and instead he sees "the self" (or "self-dynamism")
as the self-registering index of the ways in which a person
feels he has been treated, or regarded, by other people who
are important to him because of his need of their services and
love. The normal feeling tone of the organism is euphoric,
but physical depletions and felt disapprovals create tension
and anxiety. Unless these can be worked out in an atmosphere of love and rationality, the "self-system" becomes distorted and develops false or "parataxic" relations with
others. These may vary in wide degree, from the mild anxiety neuroses to outright psychosis.

The human quandary arises in the ordeal of growing up.
If a child were loved, consistently and intelligently by the
significant persons in his environment, if his needs for satisfactions and securities were reasonably cared for, he would,
in Sullivan's view, pass through the successive phases of
psychogenetic development without serious harm and
emerge as a mature, productive person able to cope with the
inevitable great pressures and problems of adult living.

But this ideal end is rarely achieved, for at least two reasons. First, the child is born to parents who are not themselves fully mature, who cannot love their children wisely
and well. Second, even loving and intelligent parents must
engraft a modicum of culture into the growing child and

this requires some discrimination between culturally accept-able behavior and that which must be condemned. In any case, therefore, the child is exposed to disapprobation, which is quite likely to be "empathized" as deprecation or hostility. As for the more usual parent, whose feelings to-ward the child are ambivalent, the effort at acculturation is bound to undermine, in greater or less degree, the child's self-acceptance and self-direction.

Thus, in infancy and childhood, the primary shape is given to the "self-system" which will tend to persist throughout life. And the main forces in this molding are not biological but psychological and moral: the emotional attitudes of the significant people in the child's situation (love or hostility, respect or disrespect, rejection or sup-port). Our predicament is that, although the nisus of the organism is toward health, the social odds are stacked against it. "The stresses of life distort [people] to inferior caricatures of what they might have been."

One of Sullivan's colleagues, Erich Fromm, has supplied an explicit analysis of the human quandary seen from this general perspective of the cultural analysts. He recognizes that human life is involved, not only in the difficulties and obstacles of symmetrical growth, but also confronted by the profound and irreducible incongruities of human existence. He identifies two "existential dichotomies," "contradictions which man cannot annul but to which he can react in vari-ous ways, relative to his character and his culture."[33] The first of these is the contradiction between life and death. "All knowledge *about* death does not alter the fact that

death is not a meaningful part of life and that there is
nothing for us to do but to accept the fact of death; hence,
as far as our life is concerned, defeat."[34] The second dichot-
omy is like unto the first: the span of human life is too
short for the fulfillment of life. These negations of life are
unavoidable and they constitute the inner core of the human situation. There are many other contradictions and
dilemmas in which we are involved; Fromm calls these
"historical dichotomies." These are alterable and afford opportunity for men to use their rational and moral powers in
freedom and devotion—to mankind. But the existential dichotomies remain, unalterable, and confront man with the
uniquely *human* quandary.

> There is only one solution to his problem: to face the
> truth, to acknowledge his fundamental aloneness and soli-
> tude in a universe indifferent to his fate, to recognize that
> there is no power transcending him which can solve his prob-
> lem for him. . . . If he faces the truth without panic he will
> recognize that there is no meaning to life except the meaning
> man gives his life by the unfolding of his powers, by living
> productively.[35]

This is clear enough—except for the demonstration that
the *metaphysical* implications involved are valid. Man lives
in a quandary which confronts him as a natural and inescapable fact. It arises primarily from man's *awareness* of
the basic incongruities of the human situation.

Christians, as it seems to me, are bound to welcome the
practical wisdom and insights afforded by these various
analyses of human growth and the varieties of its distortion.

They illuminate many of the puzzles, anomalies and ambiguities in human experience, and they offer guidance not merely for dealing with neurosis but also for understanding the stresses and disorders of "normal" life as well. They underscore the reach and depth of man's problems as none of the traditional psychologies ever did and they provide an ample harvest of inductive hypotheses which require further empirical testing, refinement and practical application. These hypotheses must be tested empirically, and by the experts. We serve no good cause by an eclectic picking and choosing between this notion of Freud's and that of Jung's or Sullivan's because of preference or compatability—nor need we choose a party and a party line to follow with uncritical faithfulness. Psychotherapy is an uncommonly plastic "science," in a dynamic flux and ferment. Fixed ideas and techniques are even more inappropriate in it than in some of the stabler sciences. Christians, if they truly qualify as experts in the field, may share in the empirical process of amassing significant data and testing them both by current techniques and new ones—but only by the same canons of scientific method, since within its operative field, there is only *one* adequate method of scientific verification. The nonexperts who are, nevertheless, responsible for the counseling and guidance of people may gladly learn and apply the practical wisdom of these theories in their work with persons and in their own personal growth and maturation.

But in their reflections on man's troubles, as elsewhere, the psychotherapists have come forward with a great many notions which far exceed the reach of the scientific method.

There are many rents in the empirical curtain which let the light of the therapists' faith shine through. Sometimes, it is a question of philosophical naïveté, sometimes a confusion between description and evaluation, sometimes a simple incompletion of the process of verification. But beyond these surface blemishes, we can see in and behind the current psychotherapeutic accounts of the human quandary a common, pervasive, overriding *assumption*, both philosophical and religious in character. Fromm states it; the others presuppose it. *Man is alone in a morally neutral universe. Man is, finally, his own and only moral referent.* His quandary is mainly a matter of maladjustment in a world in which he stands as his own guide and only hope.

The man in the human quandary, as modern psychotherapy sees him, is self-authenticating. He is autarchic in nature; he construes his values and existence by his self-discovered norms. He is a being whose weal and woe are of his own making. He is, of course, a natural entity and, in that sense, dependent on the nature of which he is a part. But he need not concern himself with what is given in his existence except to identify it, since whatever it is, is given as it is. The plastic, viable factor in the human situation is man himself—man for himself. The man of psychotherapy is *secular* man: man in *this* world and *of* it, bounded by the limits of nature—even when these limits are stretched out by nature-mysticism. The human quandary is a snarl of intrapsychic and interpersonal relations. It must be understood *within* the context of this world and its resources. It must be worked out by secularist, humanistic programs.

It is worth while to point out yet once again that this is an outlook which cannot rest upon strict, empirical analysis. It is shaped by a faith—indeed, it *is* a faith, with a basic creed, and all the traits of what Tillich calls "ultimate concern."

It is fully allowable that such a faith should exist and be professed by its adherents. But a demurrer is in order when it is assumed that this secularist, humanist faith is exclusively derived from the scientific studies to which it is related—or that the Christian world view is incompatible with such a scientific enterprise. It is this assumption—this rival religious faith—which the Christian must challenge, where he finds it, and must set over against it his own witness to the Christian wisdom about God and man and the world.

This Christian challenge to religious humanism is often construed as a warfare between obscurantism, on the one side, and essential reason, on the other. Christianity is readily charged with exhibiting authoritarian tendencies, a moralistic approach to human maladjustments, and an easy refuge in revelation and mystery. The humanist psychotherapist readily presents himself as reasonable and scientific—concerned with liberating men from their anxieties, guilt and disorder. If the issue were really so clear and simple, it could be soon decided. But, thus far, at least, it remains complicated by the fact the actual results of modern psychotherapy have been somewhat less decisive than some of its exponents would seem to believe and the further fact that there is more funded and verified wisdom in the Christian message than most of its critics seem to have discovered.

In a conflict between basic faiths, real commensurables must be compared, faith with faith. And in this interaction of humanism and Christianity there stands opposed two "ultimates." For the humanist, nature is ultimate and, within the natural order, man is both measure and measurer, master of his fate, captain of his soul. For the Christian, the Living God is before and beyond and in all things: Creator, Righteous Judge, Redeemer, Sustainer—in whose love and power we live and find the meaning of our lives. Here the Christian stands where he ought to stand, not committed to the defense of the outmoded psychologies which his predecessors have borrowed and used in other times, but free to learn what and where he can from the new psychology—and free to reject the aleatory faith with which it has been largely associated.

The fact of human nonfulfillment confronts the Christian with a radically serious problem. It is, for him, a distortion of a process in which God and man are both deeply engaged: God in sovereign love and man in tragic freedom. Human existence is set in the total enterprise of God's creation. Neither nature, nor man within nature, is self-authenticating or self-contained. All life's meanings—its "givens," its quandaries, its possibilities—are all to be sought and found in the immanent action of a transcendent love from which life proceeds and to which life's destiny is turned. The significance of man's involvement in nature and society comes clear only in the light of God's disclosures of

His will to produce such a world and to realize in it the original purposes of His creation. The psychological processes which the psychotherapist can describe—and alter—operate in a context of being and value wider and deeper than can be contained in the empirical picture of the world, even though it conserves all such truth and adds a new dimension to it. Man is neither alone nor supreme in his universe. The universe is not indifferent to his fate. He is not his own final reliance. He is, first and last, God's creature, endowed with freedom-in-finiteness. His selfhood is neither an accident nor an episode. He stands, in the depths of his being, before God and over against God—a finite reagent to the infinite Agent. His existence, therefore, is complex and precarious. He is involved in the drama of life and death, aware of the unique role in which he is cast. God purposed to create a community of finite, free and rational creatures who could react to Him and to one another, in a mode of *responsibility* which is distinctive in the order of creation. God stands round the parenthesis of existence in which man lives, as Creator, Sustainer, Consummator. Man is made for sharing in such a creative and redemptive process, for he is made for faith, for commitment, for community, for love.

If this, or something like it, be man's true situation, it would follow that man's failure of fulfillment is a deeper tragedy than a deformity of the growth process. There is a human quandary which is something far worse than maladaptation or error. It is a distortion of the self's right relation to its ultimate ground, and concomitantly, with other selves. If the self were nothing more than an energy system and the ultimate ground of such a system were the natural process, nonfulfillment would be simply an aspect of the detrition of nature, a consequence of the natural prodigality which appears to "care" for the species but not for the individual. But if the human self is a transcendental real and if God is the ground and end of existence and all its values, then the failure of a self to fulfill God's purposes for him is the worst of all tragedies. This tragedy may express itself in many ways, in the psychodynamic processes of neurosis or in low-level "normalcy." But deeper than maladjustment is the human estrangement which the Christian calls *sin*, which still confronts us as *the* human quandary, even when neurosis is cured or "normalcy" made tolerable.

The secularist, humanist faith finds much in Christianity to reject; but the Christian teaching it can least abide is the doctrine of "original sin." Defects and errors there are, of course, in any life, but nothing so mysterious and denigrating as sin. For if man is a *sinner*, it means he is in relation to God—a wrong relation—estranged and alienated from the primal source of his selfhood. And such a man could not save himself nor manage his own destiny apart from God's grace. Neither nature nor society could restore him or bring him to fulfillment. If the human plight is really radical, it would take God's interventive power and love to restore man to a just and right relation to God and his fellows. But this assumes the reality of God's prime initiative in human existence—not a projected image invoked to stave off cosmic loneliness but the true and living God, whose will is our peace.

It is necessary, therefore, for any secularist, humanist religion to interpret the human quandary in such a way as to deny the notion of sin—in order to maintain consistently their denial of God. For the gist of sin, in Christian teaching, is *the human will and desire that God should not exist*[36]—and, conversely, that man should be his own supreme arbiter. The recognition of man's estrangement from God is a confession of God's righteous rule in human life and of man's radical dependence upon Him, even in the estranged relation of sin.

There have been various theories and doctrines in the history of Christian thought in search of an explanation and interpretation of sin, its forms and manifestations, and its dark shadowing of the human enterprise.[37] Some of these theories have been harsh and bleak; some sentimental and easygoing. It is not necessary here to review their complications nor to explain why one prefers the doctrines of Irenaeus and Aquinas over those of Augustine and Calvin. Most Christians would agree, I think, that Cave's summary of the common Christian teaching is broadly fair and representative:[38]

When and however there appeared on this earth a being who was not merely an animal but a man, for he had the power to make response to God, he failed to make that response; sin leads to sin and the sin of the first man has been repeated throughout the long history of our race. Sin is not merely something that mars the life of this man or that. All men are sinners; all need to be saved. Every phase of our race's life shows the effect of sin. There is a reciprocity of sin. We grow up, each one, in a society which tempts to sin, and we ourselves increase the corporate and cumulative sinfulness of the society in which we live. The story of Eden is for us a homily, not a history. It expresses in dramatic form the origin of that sin which is universal. Why sin should be universal we do not know. . . . This alone we know: we belong to a sinful race; we are sinners ourselves, and believe all men so to be. The story of the Fall is the symbol of that fall we all have made, putting our self-will before God's will, losing our true good by self-assertion.

The Christian interpretation of the human quandary passes through the levels of maladjustment and deviation in behavior to the inner focus of selfhood and our primal relation to God. Man's real difficulty—the difficulty which he cannot remedy by and for himself—lies in his estrangement from God, an estrangement which is radical in its penetration into all aspects of his existence, an estrangement which has come about because of influences that condition a man's existence but in which a man must finally acknowledge his own responsibility and share. The basic quality of this estrangement is *unfaith, mistrust*. One way or another it reflects man's unwillingness to accept and abide in his situation as finite, dependent creature. The origin of sin is man's determination to act by and for himself, not in the freedom of a finite self, but in the autarchy of an unmastered self. Sin is, therefore, literally senseless, since man is not, and cannot be, unmastered. He has a choice of masters, but any choice he makes save God is disastrous, for no other master except God alone can save for man his freedom and true good.

The actuality of freedom carries with it the strong temptation to interpret the power of freedom as the sign of infinite power. Lured by this, men surmise that they can secure themselves from the ever-present threats of insecurity by their own powers of freedom, love and reason—and thus they find it hard to trust and rely on the uncertain providence and grace of God. This is deeper than a mistake —though it is a grim misconstruction of the truth. It is rebellion against God and assertion of man's autarchy—in a world which God has made and peopled for a human community of faith and grace! This inner snarl of man's relation to reality is the font from which his other troubles take their rise. And man must still be redeemed, here in the heart of his being, even if his other problems (in neurosis or "normalcy") are in the way of being solved. Man, estranged from the ground of his being, cannot fulfill his being, or be fulfilled in it. And thus it is that the creature made by God for blessedness lives in endemic unhappiness which affects the widest and highest reaches of his intellect and virtue. Beneath the ills and tribulations of which we can complain, there is a vast, malignant, root system of sin, from which springs the sprawling mystery of moral evil and man's inhumanity to man—and to himself. The man who repudiates the authentic source of his own humanity finds the enterprise of being fully human an acute perplexity.

Man is a finite creature, bound by the irreducible limits

of existence. He is designed to live in and by faith and reliance, in acceptance of his being at the hands of God. He
has within himself, as gift and possibility, the capacity to
mature into a fulfilled person and to share in God's creative
processes. He is the child of love (God's agape and human
eros) and is made for receiving and giving love—and finding his joy and security in such love. And yet this man turns
away from love into sin. But why? Because faith *seems* to
exclude *freedom*. Man's dignity *seems* to require autarchy.
God's love *seems* an unequal relation which is none too real,
none too trustworthy.

Man's knowledge of his finiteness carries with it the intuition of *nonbeing*; the awareness of this is what Tillich
has called "the ontological shock." Reinhold Niebuhr has
described man's plight in similar fashion:

> Man, being both free and bound, both limited and limit-
> less, is anxious. . . . Anxiety is the internal precondition of
> sin. . . . Yet anxiety is not sin. . . . Anxiety, as a permanent
> concomitant of freedom, is thus both the source of creativity
> and a temptation to sin. . . . The two are inextricably bound
> together by reason of man being anxious both to realize his
> unlimited possibilities and to overcome and to hide the de-
> pendent and contingent character of his existence.[39]

The appropriate human reaction to anxiety is *faith*, basic
trust, reliance—acceptance of the human situation in
which God is working and commitment to His purposes
in the human community. But man has also another free
option: Unfaith, mistrust. This "freedom to sin" is an aspect of God's unwearied respect and concern for man's

humanity! Unfaith breeds disorder: either the chaos which flows from pride and shows itself in *polar self-love*, or in the demoralization which comes from sensuality, which is the outworking of self-abandonment. Man's true and right autonomy as a faithful child of God is rejected in favor of a plausible and false autonomy of man as his own lawgiver. The consequence in action is an *inordinate* use of our natural powers to achieve our ordinate goals. The human quandary, in the Christian view, is the deeply tragic enterprise of a man trying to direct and validate an existence founded on a lie—the aboriginal lie of man's first "tempter": "You shall be as gods."

There are obvious difficulties in accepting the Christian account of the depth and malignancy of the human quandary. It is a view readily complained of by those who believe it is a denigration of man's worth and native goodness, and who see in the concept of sin a regression to infantile attitudes toward approbation and disapprobation. Erich Fromm, for example, disapproves of Christianity because its idea of God would deprive man of his freedom and its idea of sin would spoil his natural goodness, and encourage self-humiliation.[40] Beside the objections of those for whom the Christian teaching is basically untenable, there are other objections against the Christian pessimism about "the natural man." Liberal Protestantism developed the general view that sin is essentially ignorance—that as men come really *to know* God and His love, they will love Him in return and work righteousness in His Kingdom. There is, therefore, the question as to why we should give serious attention to the historic Christian idea of man's quandary as reaching into the depths of his selfhood.

There is one observation which needs to be made even before we suggest "reasons" for the credibility of the historic Christian view. It is that argument and empirical inquiry are not likely to settle this issue decisively, *one way or the other*. It would sometimes appear that the humanists were asserting that clinical evidence and rigorous analysis had disposed of the matter—surprisingly enough, in favor of the humanist contention. They review the empirical data, then sideslip into speculative assumptions, and end by claiming the same authority for their *presuppositions* as we would allow them for their clinical propositions. But only the unobservant—or frankly partisan—will fail to note this lack of cogency. The humanist account of the quandary rests on the humanist's faith—on whatever he believes about the world and man's existence in it. Nor is he to be berated for his faith. He and the Christian alike have begun with faith as an inevitable starting point in any reflection about the prior and final questions. *Nisi credderitis, non intelligetis* ("unless you believe, you will not be able to understand") is still a sound rule for human wisdom. Prior to any rational analysis there stands a primitive belief which may be verified or altered in the analysis, but without which the analysis itself could not have been launched. Our primitive beliefs are not logical judgments, in the strict sense. They are *projects*, commitments of the self, which thrust the reason into the process of discerning order in mystery, with pre-formed categories of understanding which are confirmed or disturbed as reason builds the structure of experience. All of us are believers in search of an intelligible frame for our faith. *Fides quaerens intellectum* is simply a medieval formula for a universal human habit.

The believing psychotherapist is, therefore, to be acknowledged and his faith respected. But it is a reasonable request to make that he *confess* his faith and recognize the primitive and trans-empirical character of his basic ideas. Since he does philosophize, let him do it with due deliberation and conscientiousness; since he also does "theologize," it is better if he undertakes to set his religious ideas in self-critical order. It is never fully rational to settle crucial issues by assumption. And if the reflective psychotherapists will examine their faith and the live options of believing that exist beside it, the Christian would be confident that a fair number of them would discover that the Christian perspective is as cogent and even more profound than any naturalistic account can be.

The interpretation of the human quandary is, in fact, a corollary of one's interpretation of human existence and its ground. If the naturalist denial of God be allowed, then obviously the notion of sin as estrangement from God *is* morbid. But if God is, and is man's Creator, then man's relation to Him is the very crux of existence. And if it appears to the humanist that the Christian talk about sin is neurotic, it appears at least as clearly to the Christian that the humanist view of man's untowardness is superficial—and, thus, in grave danger of producing consequences either fatuous or desperate.

The Christian observer is impressed by the residual moral and spiritual quandaries of "normal" people and people who have been successfully treated by psychotherapy. The indeclinable problems of life and death and destiny still remain—often remain unsolved—for people who are as emotionally stable as the average therapist and as intelligent as the average philosopher. The Christian thinker is struck by the way in which men and women choose improper goals and are frustrated in their success in achieving them; as others choose proper goals but then are frustrated in their failure to achieve. Good intentions prove to be paving stones; cleverness and culture often intensify the understanding of how far short of "the glory of God" we have fallen—or any other glory we may have set our hearts upon. The Christian teacher sees that, at the very bottom, man does not love aright and since we are as and what we love, our failure here affects the inmost and the uttermost reach of life.[41]

There are problems which remain after many other problems are solved—as life remains an enterprise after health is regained. There are our treasons against love. There are our lapses from our own accepted inner imperatives of right. There are our failures to make good in our claims for existence or our demands upon it (and we cannot reduce our claims to the level of our achievement and remain human —since to be human is to be deeply moved to surpass ourselves). There is, finally, the dark shadow of incompleteness and defect which even the insensitive occasionally sense in their lives, in the presence of great goodness, or deep crisis. And these are distortions and multilations of human lives which are not explained away by the hypothesis of sin as ignorance and error. It is, rather, the *love of error*—and for this there is no rational explanation. The humanist's hope that man, for all his failings thus far, will yet master the order of reason and the art of love, and thus become the ever more adequate self-savior—this, too, is the sure sign of titanism, the favorite sin of modern man.

What difference would it make if the empirical enterprise of psychotherapy were set in the Christian context, as alternative to the naturalist-humanist setting we have described? This is an important question and deserves a conscientious answer from the psychotherapists themselves. The comments I can offer here represent a laymen's view of the matter and are, in the nature of the case, suggestive and exploratory. Still, it may be of some use to list them as proposals for criticism and revision.

I believe that, first of all, it would be discovered that psychotherapy can be as rigorously and unswervingly scientific when undertaken in a Christian context as it has ever been in the secularist world view. The basic principles of psychotherapeutic work and the primary significance of the personal aspects of the therapeutic relation would remain valid. The freedom of inquiry and the canons of verification would, of course, still stand intact and the funded wisdom of psychotherapy would still be applicable to the emotional and psychic problems of men and societies.

But, I also believe that a Christian context for psychotherapy would add new dimensions to the relation between therapist and patient which would deeply affect the basic attitudes of both to each other and to themselves. For example, it would make a difference in their interpersonal relation. The interchange between two men, in the Christian view, is never just dialogue for always there is God, compresent in every human situation. Within, beneath and beyond the therapeutic process, there is the ongoing divine process of creation, redemption and fulfillment. The atmosphere between the two persons would be permissive—but more, for it would be suffused with a consciousness of and a sharing in God's grace. The love and self-respect of the therapist would be established in his awareness of God's love and he would be conscious of God's will for men to love one another, without possession or coercion. The therapist would know the Christian meaning of humility and could, in turn, aid his patient toward new dignity and self-respect —in the light of God's righteous judgment of them both and His love which seeks to reconcile them both. The therapist's self-knowledge would be deepened and thus he could be more fully *personal* in his insight and concern. No interpersonal relation is deeply understood until it is recognized as *triadic:* we know ourselves and others through our knowledge of God's knowledge of us and His purpose to fulfill in us His design for our living which we have so disordered.

Or, again, the psychotherapist working in a Christian perspective would be able to understand and reinterpret the religious and ethical aspects of his patient's problems as the secularist never can. Every Christian counselor can report frequent instances where people in therapy have been baffled and set back because of the persistent refusal of the therapists to consider their religious ideas as anything more than psychological material—to be explained away rather than taken seriously. In most cases, it may be said, the religious ideas were distorted and were, indeed, associated with significant neurotic symptoms. But a psychotherapist, himself intelligently religious, could do far more not only to cure the neurosis but also to guide the person to a more vital and authentic religious understanding than one who conveys, either by explicit denial or implicit disparagement, the judgment that religious experience is nothing but psychological material.

It seems to me, further, that a Christian context for psychotherapy would make a considerable difference in the notion of what constitutes a cure in therapy. It would agree fully with the basic aims of the reduction of symptoms and the enhancement of the patient's capacities for rational and self-directed living. But it would not suppose that such an aim, if achieved, fully resolves the existential problems of the patient—or the therapist. Successful therapy ought to be able to bring a patient to self-knowledge, self-acceptance, self-affirmation—and probably no further. But the Christian therapist would understand that the level *beyond* therapy had still to be traversed and he would know of the resources of authentic faith and worship to help men who have come to recognize their deeper need. The person who has come to know himself must still decide about the relation of the self thus known and the ground of that self's existence and true value. It is hardly the business of the therapist to try to "convert" a patient in the terminal stages of treatment. It is certainly not his business to convey any assurance that successful therapy is a *final* solution to any ultimate human need.

It is often observed that widely different—and sometimes antipathetic—doctrines produce surprisingly similar clinical results in the hands of wise and flexible practitioners. This suggests that the deeper secret of effective therapy must lie beneath the order of the doctor's concepts and the strife of the doctor's systems.[42] Human ills require a human concern in their treatment, because there is a deeper human need for love than there is for life and health. But, by the same token, the disorders of life are rooted in the loss of man's true confidence in life and his estrangement from that love which supports all true love on which he depends. The Christian therapist would understand this and would, therefore, interpret the process between himself and his patient as quite beyond his manipulation and control—going on in the presence of God who judges as man must not judge, who redeems as man cannot redeem, whose judgments are loving and whose love is just.

It seems to me, therefore, that a Christian context for psychotherapy is more truly human and more fully humane than one which seeks to exalt man as his own savior. The Christian message has a radical pessimism concerning man's unaided virtue and reason and yet, because of its unflinching realism about man as sinner, the Christian vision of the human possibility is all the more glorious—and still as realistic. If man is no more than a complex natural entity; if he is his own judge and savior; if the world is indifferent to his fate—then, man is quite beyond redemption, in the Christian sense. His problems occur within the processes of nature and society and it is from nature and society that he will seek and find his justification, and validation for his life. The significant human group—or else humanity itself—becomes the actual arbiter and savior of the men within its orbit. But surely by now, it is plain that man, under no command save his own or his group, falls into *inhumanity*. If there is no arbiter above men, human arbitration comes with fateful regularity to a resort to coercion. Men suffer at least as much from the evil wrought by those determined to do them good as from those who openly seek to harm them. A Christian analysis of man in society would offer a more realistic and a more hopeful prospect for man than any humanist utopia.

In the actual therapeutic procedure, of course, there is very good reason not "to lug in religion." Indeed, such an intrusion would most often be premature and harmful. The religious content of the neurotic superego is typically infantile, moralistic, tainted with magic and illusion. The first, and chief, business of the therapist is to bring these distortions to the place where they can be inspected and understood by the patient, at his own pace and in his own terms. The therapeutic process begins in genuine rapport, neither ascendant-dependent nor symbiotic, and moves ahead to self-recollection and self-acceptance. But the very success of therapy poses a significant question: "After therapy, what?"

It is one of the greatest services therapy can render to bring a man to the point of raising *this* question seriously, with a positive intent to seek its answer. Psychotherapy with a Christian orientation would understand both the question and the answer in terms of estrangement and reconciliation. Each is a complex, but integral, affair. Estrangement from God means estrangement from self and one's fellows. Likewise, reconciliation to God means reconciliation within the self and in society.

In sum, therefore, the human quandary is how to become one's true self and how to live with one's fellows in responsible freedom, in the tragic situation of sin and disorder in man and society. Apart from God, and in rebellion against God (the fierce desire that God not be), man's disorder grows and feeds upon itself. No man can come to be himself fully save as he enters into the truth of having his being at God's hands and not his own. No man can live in responsible freedom, lovingly and without predation, save as his love arises as response to God's love and God's demand for righteousness and community.

Our world is a dismal show of men and women failing in their hopes and promises, turning into caricatures of their real and full existence. In such a world, psychotherapy has done much and can do more, to understand and reorder men in their disorders. But a faithful hearing and sharing of the Gospel of God in Christ reconciling this world unto Himself would surely provide us with a yet deeper and clearer look into the depths of our common plight—and so bring us nearer the threshold of our true home, where we may hear, with believing heart, that God will yet remake us into what He has all along intended us to be. Only as we come to know ourselves as known of God, and acknowledge our disorder as estrangement from Him, can we come to that contrition and reconciliation in which we may discern our real possibilities, which God has in store for those who love Him, and which He wills that we shall know and have.

CHAPTER FOUR

The Human Possibility

Man was not made to exist in quandary and can never rest therein with any deeply founded poise or satisfaction. The great poignancy of the human plight is that it is a contradiction. It does not make sense. Here is man, with a deep drive to healthy growth and maturity, arrested in development and distorted in his career. Here is man, endowed with the power of a reason congruent to reality itself, enmeshed in the tyrannies of unreason and disorder. Here is man, made to find self-knowledge and self-expression in human community, embroiled in personal and group conflict which turns society into a jungle that corrupts the very atmosphere in which human personalities emerge and mature as best they can. Here is the good earth, with ample bounty and beauty for all man's needs, turned into a shambles and a deathtrap.

Who will argue that this must be so? Who can believe that what human life exhibits is what human life really signifies? There is, in our time, a tremendous backwash of disenchantment with the roseate visions of the nineteenth-century apostles of progress and their overconfidence about human virtue and progress. Yet even the most despairing among the realists or the most resolute among the desperate cannot conclude with their negative verdict. The most explicitly "realistic" among our contemporary existentialists (e.g., Sartre, Camus, Heidegger) assure us that their unblinking, morbid gaze at the ordeal and horror of human life is the precondition for recognizing the role of freedom and decision by which man may wrest or salvage more valid meanings than would otherwise be possible in his existence in an idiot world. The uses of pessimism are finally hopeful.

Indeed, the perception of the human quandary is made possible only by some looming surmise or hope of a different possibility—really different, really possible. There can be no proper sense of tragedy—only self-pity or bitterness—save as one discriminates between what is and what might have been—and still may be. Our acknowledgment of the human quandary is also our affirmation of the human possibility, of what life really is and is meant to be. Every wisdom about life must give us counsel about life's possibilities as they really are and show us a way to their attainment.

All such wisdoms are based upon a deep, universal conviction that there is a good life for man and that we are made for it. Christianity and psychotherapy have, of necessity, faced this issue and have produced significant responses to this demand that man find his way to the fulfillment of his true existence and his real selfhood. We must consider their counsel in this matter and take note of their agreements and disagreements. Here again, we will find that the practical wisdom of the therapists is of greater relevance to the Christian message than the theoretical assumptions from which the majority of them have been working.

Psychotherapy has contributed its share toward modern man's disenchantment with himself. Freud was aware of the revolutionary effects of his explorations into the inner depths of human energy and action.[1] More than any other of the sciences, psychotherapy has demonstrated how deeply man is enmeshed in the biological order and how primitive and chaotic are the forces which drive and empower the whole range of life. In its light, we can, on the one hand, identify the illusions of the men of the Enlightenment about human rationality and social harmony, and, on the other hand, we can understand why doctrinaire attempts at the building of society by the blueprints of reason tend to produce such unintended results as the Terror of the French Revolution, the bestialities of fascism and nazism, the apalling inhumanities of collectivisms of every sort. There is a muted pathos in Freud's nostalgia for the *fin-dè-siecle* world of his young manhood[2] but few have explained more clearly why such a world vanished amid the seismic catastrophes of a new age of frank and bold unreason.

Moreover, psychotherapy has drawn our attention to the pervasive role of fantasy, pride systems and wishful thinking in the organization of our notions about the human possibility. It has produced a great deal of impressive evidence to show that, especially in morality and religion, wishful thought readily becomes a substitute gratification for action; that our religious ideas readily acquire a magical cast. This was, indeed, Freud's considered judgment of *all* religion.[3]

Psychotherapy has helped us recognize the neurotic effect of such substitutive religious "experiences"; it has pointed out the many ways in conventional religion in which wishful thinking displaces ethical action, and God is enlisted as "magic helper" or even "fairy godfather." It is a sobering but instructive experience to analyze the psychological meaning of much normal churchgoing, preaching, worship and church programs. There is denunciation of sin and approval of virtue—but with what psychological residue? There is fervent petition and earnest resolution—but to what end? There is often a warm feeling of sharing in a good cause—but this itself may be a part of a system of pious or moralistic substitutes for a real knowledge of our predicament, a real despair of our shoddy virtue, a real reliance upon the redeeming grace and maturing wisdom of God, a real commitment and discipleship in a common life of faith and grace.

Moreover, it is in psychotherapy itself that we can find the norms for our criticism of the facile and superficial exploitation of religious orecticism by the popular peddlers of dreams, nostrums and panaceas. Any man may wish for "peace of mind," "health, vigor and success" and few will despise the hope of "peace on earth, good will to men." But only the neurotic will suppose his wishes will be granted if he reads a few books and masters a few rules of self-affirmation. Every authentically religious man will witness to the abiding and transforming effects of religious faith and action. But only the terribly insecure will be much impressed by the announcement that "your religion is a wonder drug" with which you can solve all your problems—and be happy. The psychotherapists have shown us how such a cult of reassurance serves to produce substitute symptoms—to exchange one neurosis for another. Man's possibility is not to be so easily attained. Psychotherapy has, then, helped to pull off the masks men wear and has shown us the inner confusions of motive and choice by which they live. It has also helped to find the patterns of sense and meaning in this confusion, and thus to fashion the means whereby order can come out of it.

Every therapeutic procedure aims at "cure"; at the reduction of symptoms, the analysis and conscious control of etiological factors, the restoration of health, the enhancement of rational and emotional maturity. The aim of therapy is to aid a man to a new capacity for self-direction and productive interpersonal relations. In actual clinical practice, of course, this ideal aim is often whittled down in many different ways. In both formal psychotherapy and in informal counseling, therapy is not always thorough nor complete. Amelioration is often accepted as a compromise outcome— the best possible under the circumstances. But the aim of therapy remains constant—and it directs and shapes in the whole therapeutic process.

Psychotherapy stands for the full maturity of the whole human person. It must, therefore, have also some notions of the valid hopes men can have for themselves and others —and what illusory fantasies must be discarded on behalf of truth and health. It is not surprising, of course, that the psychotherapists, as a group, have not undertaken a systematic exploration of this area of their field (for it lies along the boundary between science and wisdom). But there is increasing interest in it and one can find many comments, by the way, which delineate a psychotherapeutic viewpoint on the human possibility which is, and not unexpectedly, quite congruent with their interpretation of the human quandary.

Modern psychotherapy began with the epochal discoveries of Freud of the role of the unconscious in the entire psychic life, of the mechanisms of repression, and of the techniques by which the unconscious system could be brought under the partial control of reason and reality. Freud's hopes for man were singularly ambivalent. On the one hand, he was highly confident of the power of psychoanalysis to bring men to a dynamic insight into the character and patterns of their drives and motives, and thus give them the means by which the raw, barbaric force of the id might be partially tamed and the arbitrary tyranny of the superego might be cast off. "Where id was, there let ego be!" When a man has reached the level of genital maturity, is capable of object-love, and has formed the habit of adjustment of desires to "reality" (the order of cause-and-effect), he has achieved real mastery in life and with it a significant degree of poise and contentment. This is as much as a rational man may reasonably demand; and, as for life's irrationalities and disorder, he will know how to accept them, as given, in the human situation, and thus deal with them in sober, humane fortitude. Still, at the same time, Freud became increasingly sure that the triumph of reason and love in a human life is at best an episode in a vast and inconclusive segment of an ongoing biological process. Men may become relatively more rational, more ego-determinative and social—and this is all to the good. Indeed, this *is* the good life. But looming beyond all this, there is death, for which there is, Freud thought, an instinctual preparation (*Thanatos* instinct). And, at the very center of life, there is the systematic disorder of the id. Death is the temporal end of all biological organisms and the id the timeless life force exemplified, but never exhausted, in the particular living things. The id remains— irrational and irreformable. We have already seen that, for the Freudian, the id is the transcendental nexus of the human person. We can now see how far the human possibility is determined by this fact. The id can be constrained, harnessed, made partly rational in expression, but never essentially altered. Existence is shaped by its raw hedonism and by the heartless molds of "reality" (i.e., the causal order). A reasonable man may come to know himself and his world well enough so that he can achieve a fairly stable adjustment in it for the span of his earthly days. Nevertheless, since the id remains the basic driving force, civilization is bound to breed discontent and frustration. No Caliban will ever take kindly to his Prospero. In one of his last important essays, Freud expressed his conviction that this ambivalence of existence is irreducible and the struggle between love and death goes on—till death.

There is nothing bitter about Freud's "realism" concerning the human possibility. It was, as he believed, an honest, humble reading of the facts of life. He was not one to rail against necessity. There is an occasional pathos in his reflections upon the transience of beauty and the passing of human joys and hopes. There is a certain brusqueness in his dismissal of the utopians and the pacifists with their dreams of a peaceful world. But there is also a rugged cheerfulness and a deep-running concern for human service and the ministry of healing.[4]

Both Adler and Jung were more optimistic than Freud—almost in the exact degree in which they were also more superficial. Adler believed that the will to power was the basic force in human behavior. Interpersonal relations are inherently competitive and when they are wrongly managed or evaluated they generate the anxieties of inferiority-feeling and the evasions of neurosis. But Adler retained a residue of the classical liberal doctrine of the harmony of self-interest and the interests of the community. Thus he shared the liberal optimism that men are educable and destructive conflict unnecessary. The aim of therapy is to bring people to a rational and true appraisal of themselves—their actual powers and limitations that from self-knowledge comes self-acceptance. Such people, now having a new maturity in their attitudes toward self and others, can find an adequate expression of their power drives and need-for-status in collaboration rather than competition and conflict.[5] This is the human possibility—and it bears a startling resemblance to the theory of moral harmony in Adam Smith's *Theory of Moral Sentiments*.[6]

Jung is even more hopeful than Adler as to what man can

become because of his gnostic vision of mankind's participation in what he called the collective unconscious. Each person is connected, in his deep memories, dreams and myths, to the vast, pervasive *anima mundi*, and this tie remains unbroken even in neurotic disorder. The aim of therapy, for Jung, is to lead his patients back into conscious and understanding participation in this rich heritage of the human spirit, to find their souls in the soul of mankind, and thus to share productively in both the commonplace and the mystery of existence. Men need a religious frame of reference and this must include in it the universal myths and symbols of natural existence. It must afford to man his legacy from the unconscious wisdom of the race. Such a person would attain a nice equilibrium of all the main psychic forces: thinking, feeling, sensation and intuition. The fully realized person is a well-balanced composite of the basic psychological vectors: anima, animus, intraversion, extraversion. Dr. Clara Thompson, in her history of psychoanalysis, comments on the Jungian perspective thus:[7]

> As the Jungian school has developed, the process of cure has tended to become rigid and ritualized, and patients are said to go through various stages until they finally reach self-realization. One cannot achieve this until after middle life. The system as it stands today has the quality of a religion. Jung believed that people needed a religious attitude, by which he seems to mean a respect for the dignity of human life and a belief that it has meaning.

Jung's resolute emphasis upon life's transcendental meaning does not, however, amount to a theistic religious world view. Jung's religion is Gnosticism—immanentist and mystical. Jung recognized, in religious phenomena, the signs of "supra-personal forces which wield a fate-like power over our lives." These are forces of the unconscious: "the aggregate of all psychic events occurring *beyond consciousness*, where the lowest is one with the highest, and where we reach the end of all knowledge and nothing remains for us but to marvel at the sublime."[8] We may recognize in this panpsychic gnosticism a resurgence of that ancient Gothic nature religion which, in an age of cultural deterioration, finds a new *temenos* among the rootless intellectuals who are seeking a nonbiblical religion which does not threaten their human sense of autarchy. Jung's "modern man in search of a soul" is hardly a pilgrimage toward the Judeo-Christian faith in God-Creator, Redeemer and Consummator.

If this were a history rather than an appraisal of ideas, there would be value and need for a summary exposition of the rest of the significant psychological theorists who have pondered the question of the ends of human life and proposed their judgments about the goals and prospects of mankind. Among many others, it would be interesting to review the theories of such men as Rank and Reich, Fenichel and Berg, Alexander and French, Masserman and Rogers. But it will serve our present purpose if we confine our survey to three of the cultural analysts who represent a marked development beyond Freud and his most famous American dissenters: Sullivan, Horney and Fromm. Such a choice is justified partly because this trio has taken our problem more directly into view than most of the others and partly because their common theory of interpersonal relations has more points of contact with Christian notions than any other single perspective in modern psychotherapy. I record in passing my own testimony that the general psychological theory they speak for has been confirmed in my own experience as the most empirically plausible, the most practically useful in the sort of lay counseling a Christian pastor and teacher may do. There are, as it seems to me, remarkable affinities between the ethical and personal concerns of these cultural analysts and the Christian ethical teacher. (See below, Chapter Five.)

We have seen that Sullivan regarded psychiatry as "the science of *inter*personal relations" and, although he used this phrase in a very special sense, he did, in fact, include within his purview the widest reaches of human experience which he thought he could observe. He was stubbornly indifferent to metaphysics and to the ethical questions which clustered around his clinical hypotheses—yet he had a deep concern for what men might become. His work with schizophrenics is only part of a life of devotion not only to his medical art but also to the social and political issues which disturb society and its members.[9] He was a sort of secular saint—though he would have fiercely scorned any such praise. He believed that every man, however disordered, has in himself already the makings of a better self—a self more rationally related to others' selves and therefore more rational and productive. The goal of therapy is the overcoming of this "parataxic distortions" in one's relations with others, so that a person might come to know himself as he is actually known by other significant people and to act in terms of knowledge rather than fantasy and illusion.[10] Authentic self-knowledge is the open way to self-fulfillment. But self-knowledge requires recognition and approval by others. It is the love of others which energizes the self-system in its discovery of self-significance. To achieve his true potential, a man needs must receive and give tenderness, must enter into what Sullivan called "the quiet miracle" of being loved and loving in return. Despite his disavowals, there are overtones in Sullivan of an ethical motif which is very familiar to Christian readers, who know that human love is a reaction to love which comes to us from beyond ourselves.

Sullivan made a crucial distinction between the biological and the personal relations of human beings. He identified the lust dynamism as the core of the biological syndrome, which attends to nature's demands for the continuity of the species. But he saw something more in human relations, and he called it love, without embarrassment or sentimentalism. Love is a person's concern for another's actual good; it is what happens "when someone else begins to be as significant as oneself." "The relatively uncomplicated experience of love is entirely ennobling. Sympathy flows from it. Tolerance as a respect for people—not as an intellectual detachment from prejudice—follows it like a bright shadow."[11]

Love begets love. Honest approbation provides needed security for the self-system; it aids that self-acceptance which guides self-knowledge. With sufficient tenderness, love and honest knowledge, a human person would grow up knowing himself loved and supported and would thereby be empowered to love and enter into interpersonal relations which were syntactic (i.e., rational) and productive. He would, in sum, be sane. This is the human possibility. It is not merely desirable but is actually possible for men. And it was Sullivan's most devout faith that psychiatry, as he conceived it, was a major resource for helping people to this kind of sanity in our time.

Karen Horney was the leader of a different "school" among the cultural analysts[12] which concentrates upon the immediate stressful situation of the neurotic, to the relative neglect of the genetic development of psychological character. Her work was dominated by a deep moral concern for human freedom and fulfillment, the chief resources for which are the inner drive to health and an interpersonal relation of understanding and love.

> The way toward this goal (of self-realization) is an ever increasing awareness and understanding of ourselves. Self-knowledge, then, is not an aim in itself, but a means of liberating the forces of spontaneous growth. . . . Whether for ourselves or for others, the ideal is the liberation and cultivation of the forces which lead to self-realization.[13]

The main obstruction to such symmetrical growth is what Horney calls "the pride-system" which a person develops under the pressure of the ideals and values imposed on him by society and stimulated by his own fantasies of perfection. He builds up "an idealized self" (the wonderful person one would like to be—or supposes others would be impressed by). This may have little to do with one's actual self and may flagrantly contradict the concrete limitations of one's particular situation. But the neurotic prefers to cling to his orectic vision rather than "accept himself as a human being with all the general limitations this implies." The aim of therapy is to aid people toward a rational self-acceptance, neither prideful nor derogatory.

> The neurotic is after all a magician living by his magic powers. Any step toward self-realization means relinquishing these powers and living by his existing resources. But as he realizes that he can in fact live without such illusions, and even live better without them, he gains faith in himself.[14]

Horney concludes with an ideal description of what human self-realization involves:

> With regard to himself it means striving toward a clearer and deeper experiencing of his feelings, wishes, and beliefs; toward a greater ability to tap his resources and to use them for constructive ends; toward a clearer perception of his direction in life, with the assumption of responsibility for himself and his decisions. With regard to others it means his striving toward relating himself to others with his genuine feelings; toward respecting them as individuals in their own right and with their own peculiarities; toward developing a spirit of mutuality (instead of using them as a means to an end). With regard to work it means that the work itself will become more important to him than the satisfaction of his pride or vanity and that he will aim at realizing and developing his special gifts and at becoming more productive.[15]

So to realize one's actual powers and satisfactions, so to live without illusion, with confidence and courage—this is the human possibility, the highest and best end to which human life may come.

Erich Fromm is yet another pioneer among the cultural analysts, and of them all, he has given the most explicit attention to the ethical and religious implications of psychological theory. He is keenly aware of the general significance of the interaction between persons and their cultural stimuli but he has singled out the complex problem of authority and freedom as the prism through which we may refract and study the forces which distort and frustrate proper human growth.

The human infant is at the mercy of persons and institutions which exercise authority and arbitrary power over him. Yet his reaction to them has a kind of primitive, spontaneous quality of freedom and self-determination which means that he is not merely passive to external direction. As the pressures and stress of his dependent situation build up, the growing child loses his desire to be simply and literally himself and comes to accept the images imposed upon him by the authoritarian figures in his environment. The result is a subnormal psychological character (dependent on external props, sanctions and authority for the very basis of life itself). His innate powers of self-determination are diminished, and he even becomes *afraid* of his freedom, since he cannot suppose that self-reliance is really possible. It comes to appear less valid than self-dependence on parents, society or God. In the same way his love relations with other persons come to be corrupted. He supposes that their love is conditional and that his right to be loved depends on their arbitrary approval and estimate of him. This distorts his power to love himself properly and he develops a bad conscience toward himself and spurious emotional bonds with others.

There are many forms which this process of self-disfiguration may take—and Fromm has worked out an interesting typology of "the unproductive personality." He points to what he calls "the receptive orientation" (a close analogue to Freud's oral-sucking type), in which the person relies on help from the outside, the magic helper who will satisfy their wants in return for slavish adulation and submission.[16] There is, second, what Fromm calls "the exploitative orientation" (similar to Freud's oral-biting type), in which the person has come to expect little from others in the way of bounty but rather attempts to make his way by cunning and manipulation. A third type he calls "the hoarding orientation" (Freud's "anal-sadistic") in which personal security is aimed at by essential stinginess, taking in all one can get and giving out as little as one must in return. Finally, Fromm delineates a type he labels as "the marketing orientation" (and for this there is no analogue in Freud). This is the disposition to value oneself at the valuation given in the market place for one's services or use. Fromm gives us a very penetrating and significant indictment of a plutocratic culture in which men are hucksters and their principal stock-in-trade is—themselves!

But all these are distortions and deprivations of what is

possible for human development and fulfillment. Men can and ought to grow into what Fromm calls "the productive orientation." His delineation of this ideal possibility is somewhat more abstract than his descriptions of the faulty types:

> The "productive orientation" of personality refers to a fundamental attitude, *a mode of relatedness* in all realms of human experience. It covers mental, emotional and sensory responses to others, to oneself, and to things. Productiveness is man's ability to use his powers and to realize the potentialities inherent in him. If we say *he* must use *his* powers we imply that he must be free and not dependent on someone who controls his powers. We imply, furthermore, that he is guided by reason, since he can make use of his powers only if he knows what they are, how to use them, and what to use them for. Productiveness means that he experiences himself as the embodiment of his powers and as the "actor"; that he feels himself one with his powers and at the same time that they are not masked or alienated from him. . . . Productiveness is an attitude which every human being is capable of, unless he is mentally and emotionally crippled. . . . Productiveness is man's realization of the potentialities characteristic of him, the use of his *powers*. . . . With his power of reason he can penetrate the surface of phenomena and understand their essense. With his power of love he can break through the wall which separates one person from another. With his power of imagination he can visualize things not yet existing; he can plan and thus begin to create.[17]

Such a fully developed person could incorporate the other orientations in a noncrippling fashion. He would be able to receive gifts with grace, appropriate needful things as they are actually available, save without stinginess and exchange without servility. He would "be able to follow authority, guide others, to be alone, and to assert himself."[18]

Something like this is the true human possibility and is the proper goal of all rational human striving. But it requires an ethic and a religion. The only appropriate ethic is one of freedom and responsibility and the only valid religion is one of devotion to humanity. In his emphasis upon the moral issues in interpersonal relations and his ardent religious feeling for humanity, Fromm often surprises laymen who have in mind the popular stereotype of the amoralistic psychiatrist. I still recall vividly an incident which happened during a forum sponsored by a national picture-news weekly on "The Pursuit of Happiness." In the course of a rather confused discussion, a noted public opinion analyst offered the rather blunt dictum that the problem of the pursuit of happiness could be readily solved if people were assured that they would be protected against indigence in their old age and could be persuaded that sex was not a moral but merely a biological matter. While I was clearing my throat and assorting my somewhat startled wits to comment on this provocative panacea, Dr. Fromm rushed in ahead of us all and delivered a brief but quite definitive lecture on the *psychological* disabilities produced by irresponsible and promiscuous sexuality.

But Fromm's ideas of religion are based on very different assumptions from those of the Judeo-Christian tradition with whose practical ethical notions he has so much in common. In *Psychoanalysis and Religion,* he has outlined his ideas of the religion of humanity which he believes are compatible with our psychological wisdom and which will serve men in their strivings for self-realization and productivity. To begin with, the warrant for religion lies in its necessity. "There is no one," he says, "without a religious need, a need to have a frame of orientation and an object of devotion."[19] But not all religion is good for men. Much of it is, in fact, psychologically harmful.

Bad religion is authoritarian religion—the authoritarian element in it is what makes it bad. For his definition of authoritarian religion, Fromm borrows the Oxford English Dictionary's definition of *theistic* religion:[20] "Religion is the recognition on the part of man of some higher unseen power as having control of his destiny and as being entitled to obedience, reverence and worship." Ignoring all questions as to the possible existence of some such "power," Fromm proceeds to argue that any such conception of man's contingency is inimical to man's freedom and self-determination. The fatal defect in any religion which acknowledges God as man's ground and end is that it necessarily implies "the surrender of man to a power transcending men."[21] Such a surrender transfers the conflict between man's freedom and arbitrary power from the social to the cosmic order and is even a bit the worse for its enlarging the dimensions of servile action.

It is one thing to recognize one's dependence and limitations, and it is something entirely different to indulge in this dependence, to worship the forces on which one depends. To understand realistically and soberly how limited our power is is an essential part of wisdom and of maturity; to worship it is masochistic and self-destructive."[22]

Humanistic religion celebrates "man's own powers" and his capacities for self-realization. He can come to adjust to "the existential dichotomies" of death and the anomalies of nature. His devotion to humanity helps to guide and purify his respect for truth and instructs him in his powers and his limitations. Such a faith evokes man's power of loving others as himself and generates the experience of what Fromm calls "the solidarity of all living things." In humanistic religion man's virtue is not obedience to a higher law or power, as in authoritarian religion; it is, rather, the emancipation of spontaneous self-expression in freedom and responsibility. Faith is not assent to doctrines nor the acceptance of authoritarian teaching; it is, essentially, self-reliance and the confidence that truth must come from within one's own experience, judgment and commitment. Authoritarian religion, as Fromm sees it, produces a prevailing mood of abasement, guilt and remorse. In the religion of humanity, the normal mood is joy and confident hope in what man can make of his situation in this world. Moreover, the humanist believer can still use the term God, "not as a symbol of power over man but of man's own powers."[23]

Surveying the history of Western culture, Fromm came to regard Christianity as the prime instance of authoritarian religion—and within Christianity, he views Calvinism with an especial psychiatric distaste. He sees a fateful parallel between Calvin's concept of divine sovereignty and the modern authoritarian police states. "Their [common] spirit is one of submission to power and lack of love and respect for the individual person."[24] Humanistic religion, on the other hand, has a wider and much more wholesome record to show. Fromm illustrates this by a brief survey of "early Buddhism, Taoism, the teachings of Isaiah, Jesus, Socrates, Spinoza, certain trends in Jewish and Christian mysticism, the religion of Reason of the French Revolution." In another place, he says: "The human reality underlying the teachings of Buddha, Isaiah, Christ, Socrates or Spinoza is essentially the same. It is determined by the striving for love, truth and justice." The fact that some of his exemplars based their concern for love, truth and justice on their faith in a power beyond nature and man's powers—and some of them were rather explicit about their belief in God and His purposes—does not affect Fromm's argument. Such beliefs are merely psychological material and do not contribute anything needful or positive to his thesis.

Humanistic religion and the aims of psychotherapy come near to convergence, in Fromm's conception of them. He speaks of the psychotherapist as "a physician of the soul." Better than the priests and ministers of authoritarian religion, a devout psychotherapist could help men toward their highest possible plane: "an attitude in which life is devoted to the realization of the highest principles of life, those of love and reason, to the aim of becoming what he potentially is, a being made in the likeness of God"—"God" being still understood as the symbol of humanity's powers of self-realization.

Dr. Fromm has gone further than any other psychotherapist I know in working out the structure of a religion of secular man, as a real alternative and rival of historic Christianity. He has followed out the naturalistic presuppositions which we have seen widely implicit in much psychotherapeutic doctrine to their explicit and positive conclusions —for naturalists must have their devotions, too. But Fromm is by no means a solitary prophet of humanism or critic of Christianity. For example, Marjorie Brierley in *Trends in Psychoanalysis* concedes that "it is far from evident that assumptions of Christianity's rapid demise are correct." But she maintains that "the mode of personal integration offered by Christianity is inherently unstable" and goes on to expound "the Lebensanschauung implicit in psychoanalysis" which she calls "neo-realistic humanism."[25] This, she believes, offers a superior morality as well as psychology to anything she sees in Christianity. J. C. Flugel in an important book on psychological ethics has weighed Christianity, found it wanting, and gone on to confess his own humanistic faith. "The religion of humanity," he believes, "is surely the religion of the nearer future."[26] And to these samples, many more of similar import could be added.

For all their differences, we can scarcely miss the one dominant motif in all these ideas of human destiny. It is the firm conviction that all distinctively human meanings and values in life are supplied by man himself. The human possibility is man's achievement in a natural process which is essentially impersonal. It might even be said to be *indifferent* to anything more than the evolutionary processes of organic life. Within this natural order, if they are sufficiently free and rational and unabused, men can mature into at least a brief span of rational, benevolent and productive living. In such sanity, they may gain the confidence and wisdom both to live and to suffer extinction. They require no God whose sovereign wisdom and love are the font and ground of existence—indeed, they do better to be rid of such an overriding power. They need no redemption from their sins and guilt; indeed, such notions are disabling and obstruct the healing work of proper "loving care for one's self." They need no church or cultus of worship and common life. They *do* need psychotherapy but only to open the doors for them to enter, by their own true power, into life's largest room of freedom and sufficiency.

There is no need for the Christian interested in appropriating as much help from psychotherapy as possible to bellow with apologetic rage at this massive derogation of the Christian wisdom. Nor need he quake in anxious fear lest the new wisdom should drive the old before it. But it is important that he make the consistent and firm distinction between the practical guidance and insight which psychotherapy affords and the challenge and claims of this quasi-scientific humanism which has come to be so closely associated with the development of modern psychotherapy.

There is no use denying that much of what has passed for Christian preaching, spiritual direction and ecclesiastical influence in society has been authoritarian, intolerant, hieratical. It ought to be plain enough, even to the defenders of the faith, that all too often, in the attempt to bring men to genuine contrition and faith, some Christians have denigrated human nature to a degree which does suggest a sadistic attitude. An old back-country theologian with whom I once worked used to remark: "Now, that doctrine of total depravity, rightly understood, is sound enough—it's just a denial of the claims of self-righteousness. But some folks have topped it with a doctrine of *tee-total* depravity— and that's heretical!" Moreover, Christians have sometimes, in their zeal for revelation, demanded a sacrificial offering of the human mind—and this has been rightly rejected by the rationalists, for the wrong reasons. And, to make a fourth candid admission, it ought not to have required psychotherapy's criticism of Christianity for Christians to recognize the degree to which much of the so-called "common life" in Christian churches is, in psychological effect, the mutual propping-up of sagging egos in neurotic symbiosis.

On the positive side, Christians may readily grant the general psychotherapeutic claim that only in what is sometimes called "the permissive atmosphere"—an interpersonal situation characterized by honest respect, unfeigned love and ungrudging freedom—only thus can therapy or counseling be trusted to produce a significant outcome. Christians also have a doctrine of interpersonal relations, which deplores the manipulation of persons (even "for their own good"), and which rejoices in "the *liberty* in which Christ has made us *free*." Conventional Christian pastoral theology has much to learn from psychotherapy's critique of moralism, self-reference and magical displacements in dealing with people conscious of their spiritual

need and moral disorder. Most of all—and hardest, too—
we need to grow into an active confidence in the curative
forces at work in persons and society—even in the midst of
disorder and abuse—and we need to learn to rely upon
these residual and therapeutic powers, whether as therapist,
minister or priest. We must, presently, ask further questions about the source and nature of these forces, but at the
moment it is important to reiterate the significance of this
basic attitude toward persons, which is possible only if it is
also matched by a congruent attitude toward one's own self
and its maturation.

As he looks at the ethical aspects of psychotherapy, the
Christian thinker might very well be impressed by the insistence that growth toward the best can only follow knowledge of the worst. From this we can understand why all
therapies based primarily upon support, reassurance and ad-
vice are superficial and harmful. We can see why accurate
diagnosis does not suffice, especially if it is offered in an arbitrary or pontifical manner. It is only as a person, conscious of his disorder, comes to see, for himself, the shape
of that disorder, and the psychodynamic patterns at work
in his life, that he can come to true knowledge of his actual
situation, enabled to form a fair estimate of it. To know
oneself as one really is—this is the precondition to all cure,
and growth and maturation. The Christian further recognizes in this emphasis on self-knowledge a close similarity
of the Christian demand that men come to God in genuine
contrition—that is, without the illusions of merit or even
the pride of spectacular demerit.

The Christian, then, may very well acknowledge and gratefully receive the practical services of psychotherapy in keeping people away from their psychic disabilities and toward their actual, productive possibilities. But he must then stand ready to face the challenge of the rival faith which, as we have seen, is so often the context for psychotherapeutic thought. He must consider the charge that Christianity produces, in actual results, an inferior pattern of personality organization and that the Christian world view is psychologically invalid. He must weigh the claim that a humanistic religion and ethic is able to take up into it itself and conserve the real values of the Christian wisdom while it rightly discards the psychological disvalues which are so apparent.

If the Christian wisdom were as harmful as Fromm and Flugel and Brierley allege, we should all have seriously to consider the choice of abandoning it. In the name of our commitment to the essential biblical faith, we should have to reject any wisdom about life which inevitably and systematically distorts the evident design of human existence. If "the religion of humanity" were, in actual results, as vital and valid as its devotees affirm, we should all have seriously to consider the choice of adopting it. For at least one of the basic justifications of any religious faith is that it affords the widest, deepest, truest wisdom concerning both the ends and means of human life.

Such a choice, however, cannot be made simply by direct appeal to the authority of science or dogma. The humanist faith greatly exceeds any warrant of scientific authority, and the Christian dogmas are expressly founded upon prior choices of faith. Thus, the matter lies quite beyond the range of coercive demonstration. We come then to the persuasive force of sincere witness to one's faith, which makes no other demands than that it be considered with utmost seriousness and that a decision be made in full knowledge that it is the meaning of life and death that hangs in the balance and not mere rival opinions.

The secularist, humanist faith maintains that all the crucial questions of the meaning and value of life lie *inside* the *parenthesis of being* which is the locus of birth and growth and death. The Christian faith focuses the question of life's meaning *on the parenthesis itself*. Whatever life means and whatever final quality it may have must, therefore, be derived from the relation between man and the reality on which he does, in fact, depend—the finite on the infinite. Fromm contends that men may acknowledge the fact of their dependence without any corresponding need for insight into the nature and disposition of the reality involved.[27] Further, he claims that "clinical examination of masochistic character traits" supports his view that "to worship the forces on which one depends" is "masochistic and self-destructive." He must know that this is an illicit appeal to fragmentary evidence unless he can show that all such worship is invariably masochistic and that the humanist attitude toward the given is invariably nonneurotic. Indeed, one might more reasonably contend that men do—and must—worship that upon which they *believe* they depend. This is, in fact, what worship is: Man's acknowledgment and celebration of his fundamental reliance on what he takes to be reliable, his trust in what he takes to be trustworthy, his devotion to what he takes to be the shaping forces of his destiny. Thus, in humanism, man may refuse to worship God *or* nature. Thus he proclaims his faith that God does not exist and that nature is not man's final arbiter. But he still will worship that on which he *does* rely—humanity and himself! Christians, similarly, worship that on which, as they believe, they and all existence depend—the Living God, who bounds life with the parentheses of finite limitations but who is Himself boundless in His power and love.

In the Christian view, the basic fault of the humanist account of the human possibility is that all the meanings and values which may be achieved in human life stand surrounded by a bracket of inexorable, inscrutable *givenness*. "The development of the self is never completed; even under the best conditions only part of man's potentialities is realized. Man always dies before he is fully born."[28] Is this not, finally, a verdict of ultimate meaningless on life: that it should produce beings capable of self-realization in a process which finally negates the total enterprise? Nature, conceived as the ultimate context or process of existence, is itself without meaning or purpose beyond the infinite occurrence of life items in a dynamic system which defies further explanation—or inquiry. A human life, which by dint of good use of rational and moral powers (themselves "given," without further explanation) has enjoyed a brief episode of insight and productivity, must then, *of necessity* (also unexplained) dissolve back into the nonbeing from which the whole occurrence-sequence is continually renewed.

The Christian is bound to claim that this is simply and literally unintelligible. It makes no sense of the process of existence and the role in it of the rational structures and objective values which men can discern and verify. It disregards the problems of origin and cause, purpose and end— all of which require an answer if one is to talk of structure and value. It makes no sense of the existential issues men decide in their living or dying—for it points to events but not to an end or ground in which the meaning of these events is gathered up, or focused.

Nature is not intelligible in and of itself. It cannot be interpreted as a final and comprehensive frame of reference. Man's existence as an item-in-nature is no more intelligible in itself than is nature. If nature's final meaning is *occurrence*, then human life can find no higher meaning for itself than as an instance of this endless occurrence. One lives, one dies—the tense thereafter is past! But what then of reason in its service to man in improving the quality (and duration!) of his existence? It would seem, in fact, to be delusive, since reason works with an eye toward its vision of the ultimate and the whole.

The Christian message holds that life has meaning and value in and beyond the *occurrence* of this life or that. Life is more than coming to be and passing away. The parenthesis of finite being is surrounded by the mystery and fullness of infinite being. The meaning and value of life come from the intent and purpose in the production of life. If it just happened—then this is the sum of its meaning and value. But if human life is the crown of God's creation and if "the end for which God created the world" is His love of being, then it is a part of a grand design that contingent being should come to be and should actualize its possibilities in space-time and history—and beyond. Man is in nature—an item in the natural process—but it is his unique power and task to transcend nature in the exercise of his reason, his freedom and his love. To him God discloses something of the knowledge of creation as a divine project—and with this knowledge the freedom to participate in creation as a human project.

Man is God's creature, who bears the image and stamp of God's will and purpose in his inmost self. His existence and his destiny are valued by God's love and concern, which means that the accidental and the arbitrary events of life are never final or fully meaningful in themselves. Man is finite and is, therefore, not *self*-sufficient or *self*-explanatory or *self*-fulfilled! No finite creature can be. But it is God's design for him—and, therefore, the human possibility—that he should grow up into sufficiency and fulfillment in God's providence and through his own trustful responding to God's grace. The same love that gives us being and sustains us in existence moves in us toward our true and full maturity. The primordial purpose of God remains unaltered and still empowers and directs both history and the cosmic drama. And a part of that purpose was a human community on this earth, living in the maturity of love, exercising the powers of finite freedom and rationality, with

reliant faith to buoy them up, humility to aid in self-acceptance and community, faith to bind them to God and to
their fellows, grace to purify and ennoble their self-asser-
tions. In the beginning, God projected a human community of righteousness, faith and glory. And this, in the end,
is what will come to pass—that is what, indeed, has already
begun. This is the human possibility.

We have spoken, however, of the shadow of estrangement which falls over God's project and blocks its fulfillment. The human possibility has become impossible—for
man on his own. God will not interdict man's freedom; it is
His gift to man and He will not force him into faith or virtue. But man in un-faith uses his freedom to create unfreedom, his reason to construct the idol systems by which
he thinks to save himself. And man sees God as a threat to
his freedom, because God *does* thwart man's successful use
of freedom when it is devoted to the cause of autarchy.
Faith in God, then, is never easy for men. Instead, it comes
normally in times of genuine and profound disturbance in
the self. Faith and crisis go hand in hand.

For the human possibility to become possible requires a
genuine alteration of human concern from the self and its
powers to God and His providence, from self-reliance to reliance upon God's love and grace, from fear to faith, from
self-confidence to confidence born of a new pattern of involvement in God's creative and redemptive work. This is
the Gospel's demand for conversion, for depth regeneration, for a reorientation of motive and inner dependence.
All these bring a man to a new level of self-acceptance in

God's love, in which he responds, with glad acknowledgment, to God's control of his life, in the sure confidence that such a control is *not* self-mutilating nor a loss of true dignity, but, literally, justification![29]

The Christian message proclaims the possibility of men entering into the way of abundant life that leads to fulfillment and blessedness. Beyond the pivot of life, turned by man's basic faith in God's rightful rule of existence, opens up a process of growth and maturation which is replete with crisis, ordeal and the full opportunity for the use and exercise of all human gifts. But it is a process which is everywhere sustained by the consciousness of God's grace and suffused with the quiet joys of spiritual communion. Historic Christianity, at its best, stands for and works toward the highest and fullest development of human selves, for the fulfillment of God's design in human life and history. The Christian evangel, when rightly proclaimed, emphasizes that men should, in actual relations with God and their fellows, experience genuine spontaneity of love and trust; they must come to know the meaning of justice, mercy and community (Micah 6:8). The Christian ethic is an ethic of responsibility which puts concern for persons foremost because of the abundant revelation of God's concern for all and each of His children. It aims at the transformation of culture through the mind and will and heart of Christ.[30] Christianity, at least in basic intent, is a true and integral humanism, as deeply and urgently committed to human self-fulfillment as any secular humanism can be. But it steadily maintains that the human possibility and its attainment is a project which God and man share together: God as Creator-Spirit; man the wayward creature of God's love and care.

Christianity is a religion of high hopes, of great expectations! It is confident of God's loving intent for men and of God's ultimate victory over all that would obstruct and defeat man's fulfillment. The Christian wisdom points to a power at work in life and history, beyond our full knowledge, possession or manipulation, which moves in us and draws us into its mysterious workings. It calls this power God's grace—God's intent and concern made operable in the complex web of personal life and the human community. It goes before us in all our crises, preparing our hearts for faith; it sustains us in all our doings, transforming nature into its sacramental medium; and it enables us with power and hope for life's journey through death to destiny.

There is, of course, nothing of grace that is merited or controlled by man—neither by his superior rationality nor by his superexcellent virtue nor by his self-deprecating piety. The essential quality of Christian living is an unanxious confidence in God's presence and action in life, giving meaning to all we can do with His gifts and securing the values which we have come to cherish through His love. Faith is acceptance of our being at God's hands and the dedication of our powers for service to God and humanity in this atmosphere of love and grace into which we have entered and which is already triumphantly manifest in the total event of Jesus Christ. This is the mode and manner of life which looks toward the full maturity of every individual life and of the total human community—never in indulgent love, never in disregard for the divine demands of justice, truth and righteousness, never by a magical sleight-of-hand, and thus never without ordeal and punishment for unrighteousness—but always in the sovereign eternal power of God who is not defeated by human rebellion, not appeased by human "sacrifice," not impressed by human boasting, who, out of a good and unswerving purpose, will bring His Kingdom to its consummation and us to our true completeness.

The Christian life of grace and confidence looks to the well-being of the whole man. It sets a high value upon health—of body, mind and spirit. But health is not a terminal value in and of itself. A human life is more than a biological episode. The value of health is to supply an efficient agency for the projects of the total self, to provide a fit instrument for the growth and maturation of men and women in community with others and communion with God. Beyond the goal of health, then, there is the possibility of personal fulfillment to which health is no more than an important contributing factor.

The Christian welcomes the psychological insight that selves grow and take shape in a societal matrix, that we know ourselves only as we come to know the appraisals of ourselves made by others. Thus it is that Christian life is set in the community of faith, the church, where we are accepted and known by others in the fellowship of common discipleship and worship. But no human is ever fully and truly known by other human selves and the estimate of society (even the society of the church) often lacks both truth *and* charity. It is from God "unto whom all hearts are open, all desires known and from whom no secrets are hid," that we expect that knowledge which knows us, without illusion and in honest love and infinite respect. Beyond our acceptance by other humans in a common life is the basic acceptance by God which is our true justification. God accepts us as we actually are—not the ideal self we wish we were nor the denigrated self we despise ourselves for being. It is this actual, imperfect self which we have come to know in genuine contrition, that God takes as the *object* of His transforming grace. Wherefore, *we* may accept ourselves as the *subjects* of grace.

The human possibility, the Christian feels assured, is the growth in spontaneity and vitality of man's freedom, his intelligence and his love. It is the life of *faith*, in which men rely on and relax in the dynamic action of God's creation and redemption. It is the life of *hope*, the confidence that God has the power to achieve His will and has a will of love and concern for man, even in his rebellion and self-defeat. It is the life of *love*, human love which has been called out and ennobled by God's love, who first loved us and launched this strange human enterprise on its precarious journey. The Christian life, insofar as it is authentic at all, is the maturing of "the fruit of the Spirit: love, joy, peace, patience, kindness, goodness, faithfulness, gentleness, self-control. . . ."[31] These virtues are neither private nor other-worldly. They are radically social and ethical in their import and expression. Life at this level is possible for men—be-

ginning here and now and even now being brought to its fulfillment in God's good time and way. Such a life meets all
the specifications of the psychological ideal for man—save
only their insistence that man must make his way alone, by
his own unaided power.

The human possibility, in the Christian vision of it, exceeds man's fondest dreams for himself. The utopias men
have conceived, of a heavenly city here on earth, have been
frankly patterned after the rearrangement of man's present
situation by the elimination of man's present frustrations in
life and society. For the Christian, the future is no mere extension of the past. We look ahead to a destiny given a
meaning far more valid than we could construe for ourselves, even if we undertook to imagine the perfection of
existence as we know it. The New Testament is quite insist-
ent on this point. "What no eye has seen, nor ear heard, nor
the heart of man conceived, what God has prepared for
those who love him."[32] "Beloved, we are God's children
now; it does not yet appear what we shall be, but we know
that when he appears we shall be like him, for we shall see
him as he is."[33] There are, of course, many who have taken
this as yet another utopian fantasy, a magical promise of
"pie in the sky" for the weak and defeated among the faithful. And it is a most pretentious delusion—unless it should
turn out to be true! And this is the Christian commitment
—like Pascal's famous wager—that the evidence he sees in
the New Testament, and in authentic Christian experience
throughout the ages that have already unrolled, is reliable
and real. But the possibility is not merely futuristic. If Chris-

tian testimony and experience mean anything at all, they amount to the claim that the process of converting life's potential to actuality has already begun here and now in the transformation of the Christian's inner motives, ethical sensibilities and spiritual appreciation. Christians can take no pride of accomplishment in their remaking—for the *initiative* and basic promptings come always from God to man. Moreover, they must accept, with humble and contrite hearts, their involvement in the dreadful business of corrupting the best by the merely good or the actually bad. But, without boasting or self-righteousness, they lift up their hearts in praise and joy for what God has done, and is doing, with man's share in the human enterprise of history. And they stand in firm confidence on the pragmatic evidence from the Christian community that the life of grace is not merely a seeking but a finding as well, not merely a knocking but also the experience of having life's doors open to new and richly rewarding satisfactions of growth and victory. The Christian hope is not merely a human dream—a pious refuge for the timid or the greedy—but a live, open option for all men, in this world, in this age, in our concrete existence.

But in this hope, man still remains finite. The limits of space and time and singularity press in upon him and reduce the actual possibilities in any given situation and at every existential moment. What are the prospects for human maturation and fulfillment in such a world and such a time as we live in, or may live in in any foreseeable future? Christian thinkers have divided rather sharply on this difficult and essentially speculative issue. There are those who greatly fear any prospect for man which encourages self-assurance and spiritual pride, since these are the surest ways to corrupt the spontaneity and vitality of faith. Therefore, they vigorously reject any doctrine of man's perfection in this life, even if it is claimed as a gift and action of grace. The Christian man is "justified and yet a sinner at the same time" (*simul justus et peccator*), but this is never better than a forensic relation. All human righteousness is "imputed." Men delude themselves when they work toward or have a right to expect the actual transformation of character specified by the ideal of Christian maturation—at least in this life.[34] There are many among these antiperfectionist Christians who see the hope of perfection deferred, to be looked for, as the *Westminster Catechism* has it, "in the state of glory only." The basic concern of this viewpoint (characteristic of classical Lutheran and Calvinist conceptions of grace) is to insist on the deep-linked relation between man's finiteness and his proneness to self-deception and sin. It is a view which is deeply scored by a pious skepticism of human virtue, even when effected by grace. Human life in history is fulfilled, in principle rather than in fact, by the imputation of righteousness but never in its actual impartation.

There is another, and I believe more authentic, Christian motif which sets no *a priori* limits to what God can make of man whether in this life or beyond it. This view (to be seen in the central Anglican tradition, and in a rather distinctive form in John Wesley and the early Methodists) takes sin with all seriousness but sees the victory over sin already wrought by God in Christ and the power of that victory imparted in viable germ to faithful men here and now, in this world and in actual human living. Christian salvation is a real change of heart and character and it launches a process of growth in grace which is aimed at the full maturation and stability of faith, hope and love. Such a doctrine has never claimed that mature Christians are free from errors, defects, or even the endless tension between self-assertion and the rule of God. And it readily admits that the span of human life is ordinarily not long enough to complete the process of growth to the full maturity of Christian love. But it maintains, with a higher confidence in God's grace and man's capacity for faith than the anti-perfectionists, that God *intends* to make *saints* of men, in the original and nonpejorative sense of that term. Man was made to be blessed—he was made to grow in grace "toward the fullness of the stature of the perfect man." Man's perfecting, which begins with the imparting of God's grace and favor and his own free acknowledgment and response in faith, goes on, by uneven stages and with many a lurch and stumble, toward an end which is, like our destinies themselves, in God's keeping. We do not have to know when and how we shall come to such a fulfillment; but we can be confident that it is indeed the end toward which God is drawing His human family. This is the fullness of life in the finite creature—and its prospect brings hope, humility and zest to men who are pilgrims in the earth, whose journey is not only toward, but also already in the outskirts of, the *Civitas Dei*.

The acid test of every human hope is set by the fact of death. Man dies, as every other living thing also dies, but unlike the others, man foreknows he dies. The shadow of his forthcoming and unevadable end falls over his life, confronts him with the threat of nonbeing, prompts him to decisions which reach to the very heart of his existence. Man must do something about death—the deaths of loved ones and friends and his own death. But what is there to do? One possibility is to develop ideas, with rituals and funerary practices to match, which, in effect, deny that death is real or final. This general concept of "survival" can range from the doctrines reflected in the tombs of Egypt to the Greek belief in the external existence of the soul down to the modern mortician who disposes of death with flowers, cosmetics and soft music. Another possibility is to conclude that death is indeed real and final—and face it, with calm and reasoned fortitude. This idea of "extinction" calls for courage—the courage to be and the courage not to be. This is, by and large, the attitude taken by the faithful humanist. When a man dies, "he is as completely insensible to all such things [sorrow or gladness] as any piece of earth or non-living matter. He is just exactly as non-existent as a potential human being that is unborn and unconceived."[35] Facing such a fact, rationally and calmly, men can "give of our best to the continuing affirmation of life on behalf of the greater glory of man."[36] This general view, with its show of reason and scientific authority, has been taken up by a majority of psychotherapists, without much attention to the questions about life, personal values it leaves unanswered.[37]

The Christian hope of man's attainment of his full possibility is based upon convictions which differ quite radically from either of these two notions of "survival" or "extinction." The hope of survival, as such, is of no great significance for man's moral and spiritual fulfillment. As for extinction, it means that what man becomes and has and gives and enjoys come to a final, irretrievable end at death. The "hope of heaven" based on the idea of the survival or the persistence of life beyond bodily death normally expresses itself in visions of the compensation in another world of denials and frustrations men have suffered in this. The hope of "social immortality" based on the thought of the continuation of one's influence on posterity often expresses itself in a cult of memorials of one kind or another —not unlike the Renaissance cult of fame and honor. The Christian hope, on the contrary, is based exclusively upon Christian faith in the reality and power of God's love to accomplish what God has set out to do. There are good arguments for the intelligibility and cogency of this hope—better than the humanists have ever supposed or inspected[38]— but the certitude and confidence with which it is held rests on an inner awareness of how God's grace can draw a man up onto new levels of responsiveness and responsibility, to new experiences of joy and fellowship, to new visions of God's purposes to "finish His creation."

The Christian *hope* of the future rests on the Christian

memory of God's constant, unwearied work in projecting and governing His creation and His revelation of His love and His power to conquer evil which has been made manifest in the total event of Jesus Christ. The Christian *hope* depends on the Christian *faith* that God is the ultimate orderer of life and history, that His power transcends the time series and the processes of nature, as we know them. The Christian is quite prepared to accept the medical account of death and the biological account of its function in the life cycles of animate nature. He is by no means committed to a belief in "survival" and the fantasies of heavenly compensation. The Christian hope of immortality includes a very realistic idea of death—of real extinction—but matches it with the strong affirmation that God who gave us life wills to renew it, in ways quite past finding out, but with the same consummatory love and power which we know and have shared in creation and redemption.

If the *premises* of the Christian hope are false, then the hope based on them is fatuous. We would then be of all men the most deluded. If God is not, or if He is not Creator and Redeemer, then obviously the whole Christian case falls to ruins. And if God lacks either the will or the power to renew and consummate the human projects which He has willed into existence, then it is man's lot to face defeat and nonfulfillment with as much or little courage as he can muster. But if the Christian premises are valid, the Christian hope is deathless. It moves men to expect and to seek their highest good—and to receive it through God's grace and in His presence. It warns men against pride and the lust for ease and comfort, for the human possibility is not attained without ordeal and tragedy, but by being led *through* tragedy—and death—to our share in victory—the victory of our risen Lord. The Christian hope of glory is linked closely to the Cross of Christ, to which we bring our own wills—and to the crosses of sacrifice and service we may bear for Christ's sake.

This hope is an illusion, if by illusion we mean a conviction which cannot be known to be true in advance of an existential commitment. The Christian cannot answer the question "How are the dead raised?" and is inclined to regard it as a foolish way of posing the issue (I Cor. 15:35 f.). But he is quite clear that the confident denial of the Christian hope on the basis of alleged scientific authority is not only an illusion of the same sort, but also an illicit appeal to nonexistent evidence. The issue between the Christian hope of immortality and the humanist hope of mortality is an issue of basic faith, since both hopes depend upon their primitive assumptions about nature, selfhood and God.

The psychological import of the Christian confidence in God's power and purpose to realize the possibilities wrought in man's nature ought to be of some significance to the psychotherapist. In the first place, it rejects all quietism and passive dependence on a quasi-mechanical action of God's grace. The practical conclusion of Paul's long argument for the Christian hope in I Cor. 15 is an imperative to a devoted life. "Therefore, my beloved brethren, be steadfast, immovable, always abounding in the work of the Lord, knowing that in the Lord your labor is not in vain."

In the second place, the Christian hope emancipates a man from moralistic strictures. The author of *Colossians* joins his ideal of the Christian life directly to the Christian hope of resurrection.

> Therefore let no one pass judgment on you in questions of food and drink or with regard to a festival or a new moon or a sabbath. . . . Let no one disqualify you [on his own authority]. . . . Put on them, as God's chosen ones, holy and beloved, compassion, kindness, lowliness, meekness, and patience, forbearing one another and, if one has a complaint against another, forgiving each other. . . . And above all these put on love, which binds everything together in perfect harmony. And let the peace of Christ rule in your hearts, to which indeed you were called in the one body. And be thankful.[39]

It is all too often that Christians grievously belie such a hope and fall short of such possibilities as these. This calls for repentance but it does not annul the hope or forever cancel the possibility.

A third practical corollary of this Christian confidence in fulfillment is to be seen in the fortitude of Christians in the face of the ordeal and insecurities of life. One might call the Christian message a high faith for hard times. There is much unhealthy asceticism which has developed on Christian soil—but not from Christian roots. But it is yet a fair claim that Christianity brought to the world a new kind of courage, linked to its hope and confidence in God's action in history, His breaking of sin's power and His promises of fulfillment and consummation.

Therefore, having this ministry by the mercy of God, we do not lose heart. . . . We are afflicted in every way, but not crushed; perplexed, but not driven to despair; persecuted, but not forsaken; struck down, but not destroyed. . . . We are always of good courage. . . .[40]

This is not the stoic *apatheia* nor Cicero's *tranquilitas*. It is the dramatic courage of men whose lives are set in a precarious existence, in an enterprise which calls out *all* their powers and devotion, in a community of common work and worship—whose goals and ends are secured, not by man, but by the Lord of life and destiny. There has never been an age in human history when such courage has not been productive of a very high quality of mental and moral *health*.

The wisdom of psychotherapy and the Christian wisdom agree at many points touching the human possibility. They agree that life is growth toward the goal of meaningful living and that this process of growth should not be hindered by authoritarian tyrannies and taboos. They agree that "out of the heart are the issues of life," that spontaneity and mutuality are good signs of authentic human vitality. They agree that men should be free to find strength and courage to live without servility, that they should become themselves and not copies of imposed and alien stereotypes drawn to the scale of family and societal values. In common, they teach that men deserve the experience of individual self-acceptance and self-expression, and that this requires a free assumption of responsibility and self-control in interpersonal relations. They have a common dogma that love, truth and devotion generate an atmosphere in which human character grows and is transformed—the atmosphere in which men ought to be able to live, in freedom, dignity and peace.

But there are disagreements, at other crucial points, between a humanist psychotherapy and the Christian concern for man. We may list five of these, and not stay for an extended commentary. The first is in their respective estimate of the worth and final significance of the human person. Psychological ethics sets a high value on persons—indeed, it rates them at the very top of the value scale. But this superlative estimate fails to secure for man the worth it espouses. For if the human person is a final value, how can a just judgment be reached in a basic conflict between persons? From other persons? But this means that society is more ultimate than the individual. But is society, then, the ultimate in itself? It would not appear to be, from any evidence supplied thus far in history and experience. It is a grim irony that the secularist, humanist faith of our time turns out to be a contributing element in the conflicts which afflict our world, brutalizing and dehumanizing men on a mass scale—largely because of the success of its teaching that there is no judge of men, above men and nations and abstract human rights. Wherefore, men judge for themselves, in strife and aggression, and wrack the world with their disorders. The Christian estimate of man, for all its realist insistence on man's sinful and tragic flaw, is actually higher than the humanists—if its prior belief in God is at all valid. For man, as child and image of God, is a creature of *sacred worth*, valued by God and redeemed by His love. It is God who judges men and His judgment is sternly set against any devaluation or derogation of a man by another's rating him at a lower worth—i.e., the worth of an object or a means. The worth of men before their fellows is established by the God above them all. Thus the Christian motives for justice are radical and revolutionary. They are aimed at valuing men at God's evaluation of them!

At a second point, we may notice a difference in the Christian insistence on the radical need for depth regeneration as the precondition of his self-fulfillment.

> The Christian understanding of man, with its relentless pessimism and its exaltant faith, is no ordinary utopian dream, for it sees man not merely rehoused and re-educated, but remade. It does not crudely glorify man but it sees him, even in the depths of his sin, as never for a moment alone but always with God, in whose unseen presence he lives and moves and has his being.[41]

This means that psychotherapeutic cure, important and valuable as it is, is never enough. If men are to become themselves, truly and fully, they must also find their way into the orbit of God's mercy and grace, from which they have strayed in self-exile. In any co-operative work between physician and Christian minister, the physician needs to recognize the legitimacy of the minister's concern that "cure" be understood as instrumental to yet more significant growth and development of character and selfhood.

A third difference is to be seen in the respective concepts of the principal means to human maturation. The humanistic psychotherapist will typically trust the *vis medicatrix naturae* ("the healing action of nature") for the thrust to health and development he sees in human life. But a Christian psychotherapist, knowing the meaning of grace in his own life, would recognize signs of God's prompting and revealing action in the lives of his patients. He would acknowledge the *vis medicatrix dei* ("the healing action of God") as his own deepest reliance. And, beyond this, he would understand how life nourished and repaired by the means of grace which God provides His people.

In the fourth place, psychotherapy, in a humanist context, will consistently view the organization of human society as a plastic medium, in which human foresight and planning are decisive. It will therefore breathe an optimistic air about *the future* and will busy itself with useful programs of social change, reform and progress. The Christian has no necessary quarrel with this hopeful exercise of intelligence in the ordering of life, but he will know, as part of *his* foresight, that human planning has a dreadful habit of going awry at points unforeseen, and usually unforeseeable, by the planners. He will not, therefore, discard the liberal vision of a rational and free society; but he will refocus his criticism of society at a higher level. He is himself committed, not to an ameliorative or a conservative social ethic (though many times he will make alliances on both sides), but to a radical social ethic which transcends all social achievements and undercuts men's false reliance on any given social system.

Finally, the humanistic psychotherapy is almost bound

to rest its hopes on what man can yet do for himself, if the conditions are made favorable. The Christian is (or ought to be) as anxious as any other to reduce the deprivations and denials which come to men in their common life. But his confidence in the validity and success of his ventures rests on what God has already done for man and the favorable conditions already established in which men can enter into and share in the victory over evil won by Christ.

It is by now a sort of theme song in this book that the Christian must own himself profoundly indebted to the psychotherapists for their wisdom and their clinical effectiveness—this is both an obligation and a privilege. But he will always remember why he seeks such aid, and he will be ever mindful that the practical validity of psychotherapy does not depend on the non- or anti-Christian viewpoints which a given psychotherapist may hold. He is within his rights to criticize the doctor's faith and to examine his work to see how his faith affects it.

Whether as psychotherapist, counselor, minister or whatever, we must stand firm as Christian believers, construing human existence in both its disorder and possibility in the light of our convictions and experiences of God's power and love. We must hold fast to our vocation in the general Christian ministry of reconciliation (not at all confined to the clergy). We must seek to guide men to seek their health and well-being, always in the strong assurance that it is God who works in us to give increase to every faithful human response. Our ultimate confidence is not in ourselves, nor in man or nature, but in God—who has made us for Himself and made us to be ourselves and who will not leave His work unfinished. Through the divine initiative of love and grace and the intelligent collaboration of faithful and devoted men, He will yet bring to pass the consummation of His purposes for mankind—"the communion of saints"—in which men will find their human possibilities fully realized, in faith, in love and beyond all hope.

CHAPTER FIVE

The Ordering of Life

Human life has this distinction: it is consciously and deliberately ordered toward its possibilities and ends by men themselves. There are all manner of hindrances and complications to this effort to shape life after a conscious pattern. The springs of action lie below the level of reason and deliberation. But the effort must still be made—because we are human. It is our share in the ordering of life which most deeply affects the quality of our existence and our outreach to destiny. Deeply rooted in nature and biological process as we are, our human freedom, partial as it is, thrusts us into a different relation to our environment—and to ourselves—than anything we can see in the behavior of our animal cousins. All that is distinctively and specifically *human* about our lives focuses in this mystery of self-involved decision about the right and the good—the choice of ends proper to our selfhood and the choice of means appropriate to our chosen ends. Unconscious or indeliberate action is never fully human; forced or necessitated action is not quite human, either.

The ordering of life, therefore, is a crucial task for men—

and an indeclinable one. Our freedom is finite; we are bounded on every hand by the causal order and the time sequences in which the events of our lives occur. But the possession of freedom-in-finitude creates for us the necessity of judgment and choice as to the goods we seek, the means we are willing to adopt and the consequences of our acts for ourselves and others. This is the specifically *moral situation* in which human decisions are made; the moral quality of our intentions and acts affects the quality of our total character and experience. Even if we *maintain* that human acts are predetermined, we hold our fellows accountable for their deliberate actions—and we recognize the basis on which they require responsibility on our part. Irresponsible behavior is subhuman, inhuman or pathological. This is, indeed, a large part of what we term *mis*behavior: human action which is heedless of consequence and which harms or fails to serve the human good, in others and ourselves. Personal problems always turn up in association with ethical problems; they involve questions about values and their determination; they turn on whether men are obedient to or in conflict with their inner imperatives of right and good. Human behavior, insofar as it is truly human, is good or bad, better or worse—always in relative degree and usually in a baffling mixture. It is never merely neutral, never simply amoral.

In its early phases of development, modern psychotherapy appeared to many of its critics as indifferent to ethical issues and was readily judged to be a threat to the traditional codes of customary morality. It was clear that the psychotherapist rejected *moralism* as an ethical system, and worked to overthrow the tyrannies of the superego; it appeared that he was inclined to repudiate any responsibility for moral direction and counsel in the course of therapy. And all these unconventional attitudes seemed to many conventional people as an effort to undermine the authority of the moral imperative and to encourage a relaxed and careless behavior pattern. The most candid reports of misconduct were accepted by the therapist, not only without shock or embarrassment, but also without rebuke or condemnation. The therapists themselves insisted that the chief aim of therapy is "to reduce guilt and moral conflict and to allow the freest possible use of our instinctive energies in the service of the individual and the community."[1]

To the staunch defenders of "Victorian" morality and to the bohemian protestants who defied it, this new psychological interpretation of behavior seemed revolutionary. It seemed to puritan and libertine alike a new proposal for a modern abbey of Thélème, where the single rule of the house was DO AS THOU WILT. But there was a difference. Rabelais had been confident that free and civilized men and women "possess a natural instinct that inclines them to virtue and saves them from vice."[2] Psychotherapy's new evidence, on the contrary, seemed to suggest that the deepest motive forces in human nature are unaffected by the distinction between virtue and vice.

Freud demonstrated the pervasive, amoral influence of libido in human behavior, and he further claimed, as a clinical generalization, that neurosis does not co-exist with mature and satisfactory sex experience. This led the puritans to conclude that he approved sexual license as healthful and gave the libertines grounds for rejoicing over a scientific warrant for their own rejection of conventional restraints. Much of the resistance and hostility to Freud and Freudianism arose out of a prudish revulsion against his brusque ripping off the masks by which humans conceal their sexuality and his ruthless exposure of the correlations between sexual aberration and neurosis.

There was even better reason for the popular impression that the new psychotherapy was inveterately hostile to *religious sanctions* for morality. Freud was by no means alone in his contention that religion is a sort of "universal obsessional neurosis of humanity,"[3] and that the idea of God is a human projection of parental images from which men gain the illusion of a transcendental re-enforcement of the superego's control of libido. Freud had come to be convinced that morality and character education are "abused by being subjected to religion" and believed that it would be very much "worthwhile to make the experiment of a nonreligious education."[4] By this means, he thought, the superiority of science over religion as an arbiter of morals would be established.

It ought to be unnecessary by now to stress that these popular impressions of psychotherapy and morality are false and misleading, if we consider the movement as a whole. It is, of course, quite true that psychotherapy has effectually overthrown the "Victorian" taboos about sex and has exposed the systematic hypocrisies of customary

morality. It has been a strong force in protest against moralistic patterns of character education. But, far from being
indifferent to the basic problems of ethics, many psychotherapists, from all the schools and "sects" among them, are
very much concerned and feel a strong sense of responsibility to replace the old morality with a new and better one.
And they are convinced that there *is* a morality to be derived from psychotherapeutic principles which is better,
saner, more effectual than the systems they believe have
been perpetuated and sanctified by the traditional religio-
ethical codes. Their earnest, positive aim is the development
of an *ego-syntonic ethic*, which has been freed from the
repressive and self-mutilating constrictions of "superego
morality." Such an ethic, springing from rational self-control and directed toward mature values in personal and social well-being, would be greatly useful to men in finding
the way past their quandaries to their possibilities. One of
the main driving motives in psychotherapy's zeal for a psychological ethic is the belief that it would be, in fact, a
superior morality, characterized by spontaneity and self-
direction, firmly oriented toward self-realization in a rational humane society.

Increasingly, in recent years, this ethical concern of psychotherapy has been made more and more explicit by a
wide variety of leaders in the field. J. C. Flugel's study of the
problems of the control and direction of psychic energy is
very important and quite representative.[5] He recognizes
that "man is indeed fundamentally a moral animal."[6] But
careful distinctions must be made between regressive, con-

strictive forms of moral control and the mature, progressive forms. It is important, therefore, to develop a normative pattern of growth in morals.[7]

Morality, however progressive, still remains a business of controlling and ordering psychic impulses and drives which are themselves amoral. This has been attempted, in traditional ethics, by the imposition of a social code or the invocation of "the will of God." But these are still external to the self, even when they have been introjected into the superego and are regarded as "conscience" or "moral intuition." Even a nonneurotic superego "is clearly unsuited to serve (as it is often expected to do) as the supreme court of moral appeal. . . . We must seek the ultimate solution of conflict at the higher level of reason rather than at the lower one of conscience or tradition."[8] As a powerful auxiliary in promoting this transposition of authority in ethics, religion can play a significant part, if it is *the religion of humanity*—man's devotion to the highest human good—and not the supernaturalist religions of a prescientific outlook.[9]

We have already noted the ethical concern and insights of the American cultural analysts, Horney, Fromm and Sullivan. In slightly different ways, each was concerned with the development of a system of psychological ethics. Horney believed that the principal tasks of ethics and therapy are actually one and the same: to remove or weaken the obstructive forces to human growth so that "the constructive forces of the real self have a chance to grow. . . . I aim at the individual's being able to dispense with his inner dictates altogether and to assume the direction of his life in accordance with his true wishes and beliefs."[10] She made it a point of emphasis that, in contradistinction to Freud, her system was built around the constructive and moral forces immanent in man and that her philosophy, "with all its cognizance of the tragic element in neurosis, is an optimistic one."[11]

Erich Fromm's contributions to a psychological ethic are familiar and important. He is an acute critic of conventional morality and of the idolatries of competition and success which he believes are fostered in modern society by traditional religion. For him, as for Horney, the aim of therapy is deeply ethical: "Analytic therapy is essentially an attempt to help the patient gain or regain his capacity for love." This means "ability to love productively, to love without greed, without submission or domination, to love from the fullness of his personality."[12] The word "God" can be used, Fromm allows, but only as a symbol of man's goodness and strength. "God is a symbol of all that which is in man and yet which man is not; a symbol of a spiritual reality which we can strive to realize in ourselves and yet can never describe or define."[13] Anything more objective and transcendental than this, says Fromm, is idolatry. The problem of ethics and therapy is to lead men past arguments and conflicts about the old ideas to a struggle against evils in modern society "which threaten the most precious spiritual possessions of man." The evils he mentions specifically are: "the deification of the state and of power in authoritarian countries and the deification of the machine and of success in our own culture."[14]

Sullivan talked less about ethical problems than the other two but was no less deeply concerned about an ethical orientation for modern man. "The purpose of psychiatry is the understanding of living to the end that it may be facilitated." Its aim is "reciprocal service in the evolution of ever-increasing human dignity, fraternity and opportunity."[15] Sullivan's sacrificial devotion to the causes which he believed might contribute to the sanity and peace of the world—a service in which he died prematurely and quite poor—is a notable example of a scientist for whom "truth is in order to goodness." The common features of these three systems is their rejection of moralism and their positive emphasis upon the rational direction of life and the natural upward thrust of life toward freedom, love and self-realization.

There are two other significant theorists in this area who deserve brief notice in our sketch of the range and content of ethical analysis in contemporary psychotherapy. One is Grace Stuart, whose *Conscience and Reason*[16] is an exploration of the defects of "conscience" in the control and motivation of the moral life. The other is Charles Odier, a Swiss neo-Freudian, whose *Les Deux Sources Consciente et Inconsciente de la Vie Morale*[17] is a major contribution to the psychotherapeutic analysis of ethics and religion.

Mrs. Stuart puts together several lines of psychological and anthropological study to reassert the familiar thesis that conscience is an evolutionary and societal development. It arose out of the uniquely human need for approval from one's fellows and the uniquely human anxiety in the face of disapproval (with its implied threat of rejection and non-support). For reasons unknown, the sense of evil and unacceptability outweighed the sense of belonging and approval in primitive life—and conscience emerged as a psychic mechanism for the self-imposition of the code of the tribe. Conduct which was disapproved or unacceptable came to be condemned as sin rather than error. With the sense of sin came shame and guilt, powerful weapons for censorship and inhibition. This, in Mrs. Stuart's view, was the aboriginal blunder in moral analysis which set mankind on the wrong road to neurotic morality and men have followed the road in fear, superstition and self-denigration. It is high time for a change.

> The next stage in human development, the stage which lies before us now, might well be the supersession of that division [between the good and bad segments of the human self] with a human unity which at least aspires to be as complete . . . as the animal unity out of which the division arose. And this might be done by replacing the concept of sin by that of error, and by looking on life as a process of development rather than an unending strife of factions.[18]

Conscience functions as a regulating mechanism but it is not derived from any "absolute internal knowledge of good and evil." Actually, it is an aspect of the superego which evaluates behavior in the light of the group mores which an individual acknowledges. "Its job was to make us good enough to be acceptable to our own group even if the goodness required were evil."[19] The typical conscience operates in an unduly repressive way—particularly in respect of aggression and jealousy. It demands a show of love, respect and obedience even when these are not felt nor even deserved. Thus it works, in our culture at least, to establish and re-enforce a sense of guilt and failure. These, in their turn, serve to disable and cripple us in our strivings for true goodness and belonging.

Mrs. Stuart believes that we are now at the stage of moral insight, thanks to psychotherapy, when "the modification of the super-ego" is possible. The quality of conscience can be improved in the degree in which children are loved and approved. Their unacceptable actions are to be constrained in love and their tumultuous impulses tamed by reason.[20] Life must be valued "as a work of art and a thing of beauty." Object love must come to be love of neighbor. In such a moral climate

> . . . we should at least be infinitely better than we have been so far; that loving ourselves more, we could go out to our neighbour with a deeper compassion and a warmer affection; that having found ourselves, we could afford to tolerate the found selves of other people; and that such work as fell to our share would not be an obligation but a part of our pleasure, not a propitiation of the goaded self but a willing contribution to the common weal. "Man is not yet." But if man learns to know and to handle the stuff of his life without ignorance or shame or fear, he may yet work out of it that real humanity which he has sought so long, so courageously, so tormentedly, but only so rarely found.[21]

Whatever one may think of the manifest orecticism in such an ethical program, one must recognize the deep ethical concern which finds the chief distinction between animal and human society rooted in the human sense of moral capacity and moral responsibility.

Charles Odier's analysis of the morphology and functions of the superego is considerably more thoroughgoing and realistic than Mrs. Stuart's but it springs from an equally earnest interest in the moral life proper to man. Odier believes that psychotherapy can contribute much to the transformation of irrational and disordered behavior into patterns of rational and self-directed goodness of which man is capable. He is convinced that Freud did not mean to interdict the human quest for ethical controls which would elevate life and society above its biological matrix.

> Neither the Freudian doctrine, nor the psychoanalytic method as such, closes the door in categorical and definitive fashion to the study of values. On the contrary, they actually incite their practitioners to undertake new researches and to follow out their results according to psychological principles.[22]

Odier finds a significant distinction between three terms which Freud used as roughly synonymous: *Überich* (superego), *Idealich* (ego ideal) and *Ichideal* (ideal of the ego). The first of these, he thinks, denotes a very primitive mechanism of the unconscious which emerges, psychogenetically, *before* the self-system and the capacity for self-determination begins to function. These develop in a concomitant growth with the ego and with the projected ideal of the ego (which Odier calls *l'ideal personnel*). The primitive superego is thus a separate aspect of the psychic control system, irrational, arbitrary and inhibitory. Id and superego are therefore paired off in a tension beneath the level of reason and morality. Superego control takes the form of a pseudo-morality that is, in effect, superstitious and obsessional. The only way to an authentic ethical life is to re-enforce the tendencies of the ideal of the self (*ideal personnel*) to replace the false morality of the superego (*surmoi*). As this is done, human decisions can be more firmly grounded in rational values which are established in truth and love. Morality can, and must, become an affair of conscious and deliberate choice of rational and humane values. Otherwise, the pseudo-morality of the unconscious will condemn man to the baffling frustrations of anxiety, compulsiveness and failure.

Perhaps the most striking section of Odier's book is a long *tableau comparatif*, in which he sets over against each other the differences, in development and operation, of the two antithetical systems of morality: the unconscious controls of id and superego over against the conscious controls of ego and rationally apprehended values and ideals.[23] Superego control (which is, in effect, *conventional morality*) is arbitrary, compulsive, blind. Its weapons are autopunitive: shame, guilt and self-denunciation. Its methods of release are expiatory and magical. It is static and narcissistic —it stresses a heteronomous notion of duty. It has the power of repression of unacceptable impulse, but it exercises it in a way which prevents any conscious, truly moral inspection of options and thus precludes self-knowledge and responsibility. Its notion of control is incurably authori-

tarian. Edicts and prohibitions are beyond rational judgment, so that even when defied, the superego has its revenge
in guilt and anxiety. Life lived at this level of direction is a
moral chaos, a heaving tangle of irrational impulses and restraints—a squad of blind policemen trying to quell a surging mob.

In almost direct antithesis to these negative traits of the
pseudo-morality of the superego, Odier sets down a cata-
logue of the traits and powers of a self-directed, rational
morality. This is the ethic of choice, of consciously chosen
obligations; in it the ego assumes control of impulse and
regulates it according to ethical principles. This involves
self-denial and self-restraint but the motive for such re-
nunciations comes from the freely willed and self-approved
values which are served thereby. It also involves error, mistake and failure—but these do not stir up feelings of guilt
and remorse; nor do they require self-punishment. The ego,
free to appraise the actual situation rationally, can accept
its responsibility—and can even, according to Odier, conceive of God as existing independently of the self.[24] This
makes for true autonomy, where reason and freedom act
in concert to formulate both the means and the ends of the
good life. An ego-syntonic ethic makes room for rational
concepts of duty and authority, but it controls both inner
and outer pressures by conscious and self-directed devotion
to personal and social values. Thus it is relatively free from
unconscious repression, and yet is able to judge and deal
openly with the impulses and the disturbances which still
arise in psychobiological life. Such an ethic is free, rational,

discriminative—and above all, sane and healthy. Men, living in such a fashion, would rise above "egoism" and would achieve not only self-fulfillment but would also develop a true commitment to the highest values of human existence. The common task of ethics and psycho-analysis, as Odier sees it, is the stimulation and encouragement of "conscious morality": the ego-directed, rational and responsible ethic of deliberation and devotion.

"Unconscious morality" is a "dangerous thief of values." It is, therefore, the task of psychoanalysis, education and religion to replace the superego system with the morality of conscious control and "to re-establish the conditions in which a person can acquire a positive preference for personal responsibility." A person living in free and deliberate concern for moral values would not only gain the power to deal with temptations of irresponsibility but also to discriminate between the *occasions* of temptation and the deeper drives which are the actual cause of moral crisis.

Moreover, such an ethic would comport with an intelligently conceived religious world view, according to Odier. Unconscious morality makes for an egocentric religiosity, concerned with scruples and fear, aimed principally at security, rescue from sin and religious narcissism. The ethic of conscious control conceives of the religious life as a service of the Good; "the Gospel may be interpreted as a principle of freedom and of love."[25]

Odier makes an interesting point about the sense of guilt which I have never before come across in psychotherapeutic literature. He testifies that, in his extensive analysis of neurotics suffering from violent anxieties about sin and damnation which are consciously based on their belief in the doctrines of original sin and reprobation, the self-condemning superego *precedes* and *exploits* such religious teaching, rather than is formed by them. He suggests that an ego-syntonic ethic would be able to explore and evaluate a doctrine of sin in a positive and productive fashion; whereas, in the mind dominated by a superego morality, the doctrine is distorted by the inner conflict, in which remorse and anxiety feed upon each other and make doctrines to rationalize their misery. This suggests that, whereas a superego morality appropriates and abuses religious teaching as a form of rationalization and defense, an ego-syntonic morality might freely and rationally commit itself to a rational religious perspective and to an ethical theory derived therefrom.

This brief survey of this representative sector of the field is enough to make plain the point that modern psychotherapy is developing a wide and deep concern for moral values and a high and noble vision of man's ethical well-being. The amoral drives and impulses which man shares with his brute cousins must be controlled. It is agreed that life may be ordered to good ends which enrich and fulfill personal and communal life. The power and form of this control must come from within and must be based upon valid self-knowledge, self-acceptance, self-affirmation, and it must be directed toward interpersonal relations chiefly characterized by mutuality and love. It is this power of control and direction of instinctual forces which separates man off most distinctively from his natural inheritance. The aim of human life is conquest of libido by reason and conscious purpose. From Freud's great slogan, "Where id was, there let ego be," we can move forward to Fenichel's amendment: "Where *super-ego* was, . . . there shall ego be."[26]

The psychotherapists have come to wide agreement that love is the only force that can cope with libido. It is the sovereign virtue for the prevention and cure of the distortions of life which come from the chaos of biological drives and the despotism of social taboos. A person loved and loving will come to possess the kind of health and goodness which harnesses psychic energy to productive uses, which takes the bruises and the denials of everyday living in stride, which handles lapse and failure without self-contempt, or self-abandonment.

This is indeed a lofty ideal for human living and all the more remarkable because it is maintained by men who, in their daily work, see life in all its indignity, weakness and self-destructiveness. It is no wonder then, that the immediate practical concern of psychotherapy, as far as ethical questions are involved, is the reduction of guilt and the overthrow of morbid conscience. This is often accompanied by an effort at the reshaping of the conscience and the encouragement of spontaneity and self-affirmation.

To conceive and advocate such an ego-syntonic ethic is also to assume that it is possible for man, that the hindrances which have hitherto blocked its development can be removed or overcome. If this is the good life for man, why has it not been attained—and how can man make his way up onto this new level of morality? Whence would come the power to achieve this new ordering of life? How *can* the id be tamed, the superego deposed, and love and reason triumph in human affairs where now unreason and malice wreak havoc with our hopes and dreams? What is the evidence to show that this psychological prescription for virtue is not, in fact, yet another wishful, utopian escape from the tragic reality of an ambivalent existence in which men see visions of the good society but go on living in the same house on Wistful Vista?

The psychotherapists have, of course, faced these questions and have satisfied themselves that there are honest and sound answers to them. They point to the actual changes which occur in the moral traits and dispositions of persons during the course of successful therapy. It is a fact, as they can show, that people in the process of overcoming neurosis also develop, at the same time, new capacities for self-directed judgments about themselves and other people, new impulses to tolerance and to love, new powers of self-control and nonindulgence. From this they conclude that reason and freedom are enhanced in the same degree in which instinctual controls and immature personal feelings are outgrown. Morbid anxiety and destructive guilt feelings are reduced, the habit of self-deprecation is changed to one of self-regarding criticism, guided by the new-found courage to be oneself.[27]

What holds good for moral improvement in the individual also applies, at least in part, to the family and to groups small enough to be suitable subjects for the therapeutic process. There is good evidence to show that children growing up in an atmosphere of love and respect, of nonmoralistic guidance and control, do manage to develop a higher degree of self-respect and self-direction in their interpersonal relations—appropriate to their age and experience—than children reared in authoritarian regimes. Groups in which mutuality and sincere respect are shared show a drop in dominance-aggression patterns and a rise in affirmative and complementary social experience. "Sanity" and "virtue" do correlate—and very highly at that.

To date, in a disorderly age, it is an open question whether psychotherapy can contribute as much to the recovery of sanity and virtue as the demoralization of culture is contributing to the increase of mental illness and the frustration of human dreams for peace, freedom and community. There are vast and stubborn complexes making for conflict and destructiveness in every large society in the modern world—and beyond all domestic problems the threat of international disorder seems unremitting and insoluble. Freud, as we know, was pessimistic about the prospects of the transformation of the savage forces of the unconscious. Barbarism is still too strong a residue in us; "we are all a gang of murderers at heart."[28] On the other hand, many of the leaders in the current generation of psychotherapists are not only more hopeful of what can be done, but also are rendering notable and devoted service to the cause of justice, peace and sanity in the world.[29]

But there are deeper levels in this problem of a psychological ethic which still remain unsettled, and which raise questions that lead us back into the hidden issues of moral philosophy and religious faith. We have thus returned, as in a kind of complex maze, to the prior assumptions that shape a man's ethical outlook, the presuppositions which guide our analysis and govern our basic moral convictions. They cluster around the discrepancy between the actual circumstances of our lives and the ethical vision we have of the good life. How are we to interpret the frustrations and corruptions of the good which men profess to know and serve? If our ineradicable instincts are insufficient for the direction and shape of life, where will we find the reason and the love to deal with them. It is one thing to know that virtue must needs be spontaneous and self-directed to be authentic, another thing to achieve it, and yet another thing to deal with the mysterious frustrations to virtue which we find even in the lives of the sane, the emancipated, the humane. Love is the sovereign specific for human ills; yet love cannot be legislated or evoked at will. How is it that men of mediocre performance know more of the moral precepts than the best ones practice? If human life is transformed by love, what does it take to generate love—and is human love enough to effect and maintain the transformation? Why is it that life *must* be ordered, and yet must be ordered from within the self and on behalf of the common good? What *is* the *source* of human good and how do men find and relate themselves to it? In short, what is the *power* and the *right* that impels, sustains and validates human devotion to the good?

The psychotherapist committed to the secularist-humanist faith will have an answer to these questions. Some of them will point to "Nature" and say that man is as naturally good as he is naturally healthy. Remove the constrictions of error and superstition and self-contempt and virtue will grow by its own innate viability. It is easy to see in this a new version of an ancient wisdom. The Stoics taught the Romans that "the life according to nature" was the good life. And the romantics are still contending that the natural vitalities are the pure font of true virtue and happiness. There are important modern philosophers who find in nature the thrust and support for human values. John Dewey developed both an ethics and a religious faith based on his conviction that there is a congruity between human ideals served faithfully and the inner order of natural process.[30] Henry Nelson Wieman argues for a "naturalistism" in which all human values are derived from the creative process ("creative event") which he believes he can identify and delineate quite without "recourse to any transcendental grounds, orders, causes or purposes beyond events, their qualities and relations."[31] "The creative event" can be called "God." It is clearly superhuman but not at all supernatural.[32]

But most of the psychotherapists see nature as prevailingly amoral and find the source of human good in man himself. In an important sense, man is an anomaly in nature; he is an item in the total process and yet he has the capacity for *evaluation*, which means both creating and judging values. This viewpoint interprets nature as a vast dynamic field of impersonal events and relations, in which man has emerged but which cannot be said to have "intended" or "purposed" such a creation. Mrs. Stuart has summarized this difference between the "values" of nature and the values which men create in nature:

I am using the word "nature" here—in a personification justified, I think, by its usefulness—to describe as best I can a life-principle that operates throughout the whole range of organic life including the life of man; a principle that is not only non-human in value, but often actually opposed to many of the human values which man came later to put upon his life. It is true that this life-principle has expressed itself in a beauty lavish, radiant and various; and that it has developed forms of co-operation, mutual aid, and self-sacrifice which have appealed greatly to the sentimental human mind. And indeed, even without sentimentality, the fact remains that the human social forms could not have evolved without the preceding "natural" ones. But instinctive co-operation, assistance and even devotion are profoundly different from human co-operation, succour and love.

The values of nature present themselves to us as impersonal and non-human. Nature has no concern with good and evil, kindness and cruelty, sorrow and joy. Like Caliban's "Setebos," she goes "making and marring clay at will."

> Thinketh such shows nor right nor wrong in Him
> Nor kind, nor cruel; He is strong and Lord.
> Am strong myself compared to yonder crabs
> That march now from the mountains to the sea;
> Let twenty pass, and stone the twenty-first,
> Loving not, hating not, just choosing so.
> (Robert Browning, *Caliban upon Setebos*)

So works the cancer that attacks the kind and the unkind; so the earthquake that swallows the sinner and the saint.[33]

Human good arises as men cherish one another and invest their common quest for natural satisfactions with values that depend upon their interpersonal relations.

Erich Fromm, as we have seen, differentiates sharply between the natural givenness of life and death and transience and the positive values which man can create and enjoy within the limits of existence. Nature provides for man's occurrence but is indifferent to his fate. Yet man has a capacity (whence?) to transform amoral process into authentic value. In the setting of nature, he can make a good life for himself and his fellows—the distinctively human life of "reason, love and productive work."[34] This is chiefly due to the fact that man can *understand* the pleasure-pain dynamism and so learn to *operate* it, rather than merely to react reflexively. By the power of his reason, he can evaluate, and thus order his life in a fashion far different from the rest of animate nature. But, as a concomitance of his power of reason, man also has a need for "a framework of love and devotion," i.e., an ethical and religious perspective. Life is as good as men make it. And because they can make it so much better if they are healthy and wise, Fromm becomes an evangelical apostle of a humanistic religion.

J. C. Flugel also distinguishes between nature as the matrix of man's moral experience and society as its active cause. Man is without *personal company* in an immense, impersonal system of events and processes. Human reason and love are *human* values: they are the criteria by which we know and value everything—and there is no other.[35]

We have surveyed enough of the psychological ethic to

be able to summarize their general answer to the question of the ordering of life. The main contention is that there is an innate human virtue which naturally replaces pseudo-morality with the true spontaneities of love and reason as freedom and self-knowledge are given a chance to affect the human situation. Insofar as this occurs, the conflict between instincts and society is reduced to manageable bounds. Men can analyze and estimate themselves and their interpersonal relations in the light of a friendly reason. In such a light, society's weapons of shame and rejection lose something of their terror. Instinctual drives become less irresistible and arbitrary. Persons will come into their own and human societies will become truly humane.

This psychological ethic is, first and last, an ethic of man's self-affirmation, based on his confidence in human goodness. Above all, it is the human determination to wrest a fair share of light and joy from the work of a blind, unfeeling demiurge of nature. It is the human courage to live out life's brief candlespan in dignity, zest and happiness. To be—and then not to be—and give the whole a human meaning: this is the ethical challenge and opportunity which nature offers man. And man, in his own powers and right, can rise to his challenge and exploit his opportunity.

This psychological ethic has rightly identified the main problems which any ethical system has to put in right relation. The first of these is the attainment of *dynamic self-control*, in contrast to either license or legalism. The second is the encouragement to devoted self-commitment, in contrast to sadistic or masochistic self-regard. They have demonstrated that man can make nothing properly human out of the life of passion alone, and they have made plain that the reason which gives structure and order to life has no energy of its own. Only love, which binds into one complex action the surgings of eros and the patterning of logos, can provide *control* that is dynamic and free. But self-control is not enough, since human life cannot be isolated from social stimuli and responsibility. Again, it is only love, the giving of what one has without self-abandonment or self-assertion, that can prompt self-committed service to one's fellows. The ordering of life, and with it the goodness and joy of life, come from truth and love as these are sought and manifested in human life. But this is primarily a *human* enterprise, and is promoted by men who know themselves to be the arbiters of all values. Something like this is the faith and the hope of the secular humanists among the psychotherapists; they see themselves as ministers of the religion of humanity, in which science is the chief among the means of human grace.

Such an ethical viewpoint is of great interest to Christians, who are inevitably involved in the same questions of how life is rightly ordered. We might well begin by noticing the important points of agreement and mutual re-enforcement between the humanist and the Christian ethic before we pass to an analysis of the cleavages which separate them in their prior assumptions. And, since we are more concerned with an authentic ethic than with the strife of systems, we will try to indicate the sense in which the Christian ethic can receive and contain the values of the humanist ethic as the latter cannot receive or contain an ethic grounded in Christian faith. It would be our claim that the two ethics need not finally be rivals—that the Christian ethic, with its wider and deeper dimensions of reference to God's creative and redemptive love is the fulfillment of the truth in all the human visions of the ordering of human life.

We have already stressed the agreement between the psychological and the Christian ethics in their stress on the importance of spontaneity and self-direction in all significantly ethical action. It is unhappily a fact that the ethical performance of the nominal Christians in the churches is so fully adapted to the mores of the community and the customary sanctions of society that observers from outside often fail to recognize the Christian ethic for what it is: *an ethic without a code*.[36] "The moral ideal for Christians lies not in a code, nor in a social order. It lies in a life where love to God and man is the spring of every thought and word and action."[37] The constant emphasis in Jesus' precepts is on the spontaneous energy of the faithful heart, not only for the control of unruly impulse but also for the unanxious promptings to positive goodness in love and service. He rejected all tables of moral calculation and the codes of casuistry of his time.[38] He insisted that the basic demand that men love God supremely and their neighbors mutually was not an external order, but the challenge to self-commitment to the righteous rule of God in human lives. This "Kingdom of God" stands above all taboos and rules—it is both more radical and humane than even the high-minded moralism of the Pharisees.[39] There was a momentous struggle in the primitive Christian community over the rightful authority of the Mosaic law and the codes of rabbinical Judaism for Christians, and especially, Gentile Christians. The result was the triumph of the conviction that Christianity was, in fact, a new mode of life, grounded in the liberty generated by their new relation to God in Jesus Christ. The essential sign of freedom is goodness, which springs from human love awakened and purified by the love of God. This Christian love is self-denying and yet also self-respecting; it is self-giving and yet also self-rewarding. It generates the energy for authentic virtue, neither slavish to the law nor contemptuous of it. The new morality of the Christians, in which "there is neither circumcision nor un-circumcision," springs out of an inner response of the self to God's basic claims on man's allegiance and to His un-merited love in man's redemption. The Christian ethic is the expression of the Christian faith. Faith prompts the works of love, not because they are commanded, but be-cause there is a fusion of impulse and insight which God's grace effects in Christian living.

The love born of Christian faith can be trusted to control and direct the psychic energies as nothing else can (II Cor. 5:14). The Christian understands that without the force of love, reason is impotent; without the constraint of love, pas-sion is destructive; without the sincerity of love, piety is pre-tentious (I Cor. 13).

The Christian who can distinguish essence from appear-ance in Christian ethics will, then, recognize the futility of moralism—and will know why the puritan's fears, that rules are our only defense against license, are false. He will welcome the corroborative testimony of the psychotherapists that a code is an inferior solution to the problem of ethical control. Indeed, he may find himself admitting that the psychotherapists have illuminated the age-old struggle in the Christian community between the extremes of antinomian insensitivity to the great issues of social reform and transformation and the legalistic concern to settle all moral uncertainties by the reassertion of a sort of Christian Pharisaism. The psychotherapist has a valid criticism to make of the actual residues of moral confusion which he finds in the neurotic mechanisms of his Christian patients.

The Christian will, for his part, accept psychotherapy's careful analysis of the radical difference between biological vitality and human self-control in the development of a nonascetic, spontaneous ethic. The vitalities of the human organism must be ordered by insight—they do not order themselves. The mob rule of the id is even worse than the tyranny of the superego—if the lesser of two evils must be chosen. But both the psychological and the Christian ethical views emphasize the moral superiority of self-determined nonindulgence over either self-indulgence or external restraint. Human ethics is no simple organization of the natural vitalities themselves. The good life for man is, therefore, no mere following of the ways of nature—it calls for something distinctively human: reason, devotion and self-control. Christianity has often, especially in its monastic and puritanical forms, sought to achieve control of the physical

vitalities by an ascetic repression that tended toward a con-
tempt for the body and its needs—an attitude which reflects
a deep fear that libido is too strong for self-control. Mo-
nasticism gave to life a rule and a code, of poverty, chastity
and obedience, which often (though not always) solved
the ethical problem of self-control largely by recasting it
into authoritarian terms. Similarly, the pietist has tended
to narrow the focus of the ethical conflict to the compass
of personal life and to ignore the task of remaking society
after the pattern of Christian love. And the large mass of
churchfolk, Christian in not much more than name and
registry, have been content with a complacent ethic which
assures them that their being a little (or a lot) better than
their neighbors (or the Communists) is enough to prove
God's special favor and blessing to them and their society.
There is an interesting and baffling moral acrophobia
among people and many Christians suffer from it. The ele-
vation of the concept of Christian liberty (an ethical pattern ordered from within the person) frightens them and
they feel moved to snatch their fellows back from the preci-
pice of license and to protect (actually, to overprotect)
them with laws and codes ("festivals, new moons and sab-
baths") from which an obedient Christian can learn his
duties and prohibitions. There has, indeed, been much puri-
tanism and casuistry and sado-masochism among professed
Christians—and in the name of the Christian ethic—and
many an indiscriminating observer (some of them our psychotherapeutic colleagues) has mistaken the distortion of

Christianity for its reality. Thus, they have supposed that Christianity is an authoritarian moralism and rejected it along with other ethical systems judged as inadequate.

But however instructive the psychological ethic may be to the Christian, both for correction, reproof and for positive guidance, it is finally incompatible with the Christian ethic in respect of some of its basic premises. Every ethic is an expression of a faith of some sort and the humanist faith on which the psychological ethic rests must be judged inadequate by the Christian who is seeking to ground his ethical precepts in the widest and deepest reach of faithful reason. For, at the last, he sees the choice as between man's faith in himself, as his own lawgiver and source of grace, and man's faith in God, as the source of human good, as giver and sustainer of life, the righteous judge of all men, as the power of love which triumphs over evil and tragedy.

The ethical wisdom of the psychotherapists we have studied is based on the confidence that human life transforms itself in the absence of crippling or aberrant influences and in the presence of love and rational insight. The Christian ethic is no less interested in the optimum conditions for human development but it is convinced that the transformation of life comes as an interaction of man with a reality and power beyond man, from man's response to God. The Christian evangel calls for a conversion of loyalties and reliance from self—and society—to the true Creator and Redeemer, who is before and above all human existence and value. "The kind of goodness that Jesus expects is the fruit of religious transformation, the shining of a light that has

been kindled in the heart. . . . Jesus was not so foolish as
to imagine that moral demands such as his could be fulfilled without some radical change in men's dispositions,
nor was he so devoid of faith in God and man as to despair
of the possibility of such a change."⁴⁰ It is with this basic
demand for radical change that Christianity confronts the
psychological ethic and finds there a serious disagreement
as to what and how men may find their true good.

The psychological ethic, then, is a way to the ordering of
life by the principal means of *self-affirmation.* Self-knowledge, self-acceptance, and even self-denial, are so many aspects of the basic positing of the self, the affirming of its
place and worth in existence. The Christian ethic, on the
contrary, explicitly seeks the ordering of life by means of
self-denial. Obviously, the disjunction between the two
ways is not simple or final. Self-affirmation involves self-
denial and self-denial, in the Christian way, yields, as an
uncalculated consequence, a new kind of self-affirmation.
But, for all this, there is a basic incongruity between any
ethical program of enlightened self-interest and the Christian teaching of self-denial and self-sacrifice. It is a mistake,
as we shall see, to interpret the Christian demand for self-
denial as masochism or denigration. But it is not a mistake
to see that the biblical ethic and the Christian tradition
give us a clear and unexceptional *motif* on this point.

And he called to him the multitude with his disciples, and
said to them, "If any man would come after me, let him deny
himself and take up his cross and follow me. For whoever
would save his life will lose it; and whoever loses his life for

my sake and the gospel's will save it. For what does it profit a man, to gain the whole world and forfeit his life? [41]

So therefore, whoever of you does not renounce all that he has cannot be my disciple.[42]

You are not your own; you were bought with a price. So glorify God in your body. . . . You were bought with a price; do not become slaves of men.[43]

To the self-regarding man these seem harsh imperatives and they are readily pointed to as evidence that Christianity is an inferior, morbid outlook on life compared to the healthy ethic of self-affirmation and enlightened self-interest. And, indeed, there is abundant evidence that a lot that passes for Christian self-denial is either pious or impious self-hostility, in which merit is measured by self-punishment and humility by self-deprecation. What, however, does such evidence prove? That the Christian message is very imperfectly understood and practiced by many who bear the name—a sad but not quite startling contribution to our knowledge. A closer, inward look at the Christian meaning of self-denial yields a very different conception and leads us directly to the very center of conflict between the two ethical viewpoints under review.

In a world where man is the measure of all things, and pre-eminently of human values, any radical denial of self-importance is a sort of self-mutilation. Obviously, one must not be overweening, in pride or self-assertion: but the value a man is able to place upon himself—in the light of the appraisals of others—is his value. Self-denial can only be justified as the free subordination of a self-valuing person to a value not only higher than, but also the actual ground of, human values. In a humanist ethic, there is no such value, above and beyond mankind; hence, self-denial, save as a mode of self-control, is unjustifiable. But in the Christian perspective, it is actually the case that man is a finite creature of God, who is the real source and ground of man's being and values and destiny. Self-denial, in relation to God, then, is the simplest form of realistic acknowledgment of man's true situation. To deny oneself, in the Christian sense, is not to despise or contemn the self; actually, of course, self-disparagement is an inverted form of pride. (The easy test of this is to agree with another's self-disparaging verdict on himself as if it were sincere and realistic.) True self-denial, in its simplest terms, is the deliberate repudiation of the notion that the self is infinite, or sufficient, or, in any *ultimate* sense, autonomous. Self-denial is an insightful and free acceptance of a creaturely role; it is the conscious ratification of one's *subordinate* relation to one's Creator. The other side to self-denial is obviously the affirmation of the primacy of God. This is the ethical form of the Christian confession of the reality and the sovereignty of God; it is the free obedience to the Great Commandment that we are to love God with our total selves and all our powers. To set God first is not to devalue man nor to deprive him of his proper rights and satisfactions. But it does commit a man to the acknowledgment that his gifts and powers are his own as divine endowments, to be received and exercised in faithful stewardship and service to "the neighbor" and to all mankind.

It is the Christian conviction that self-denial, rightly understood, is the master key to the right ordering of life, for
it sets first things first and provides a system of value relations in which we can judge for ourselves, in responsible
decision, as to the right and the good. It is self-appraisal of
faith, for it affirms that our selves, not ultimate in themselves, are projected into an immense and dynamic field of
God's providence, controlled in its deepest meaning and
final outcome by God's loving care for all His children and
their fulfillment. In the pivotal section of the Sermon on
the Mount, Jesus highlights the problem of human anxiety
and frustration with quite uncommon insistence (five times
in ten verses; cf. Matt. 6:25–34). His teaching is that basic
anxiety is the outworking of a self-interested love, which
puts self-concerns foremost. The way beyond anxiety is
through the abandonment of the program of self-security
and by risking oneself, as a swimmer does in water, to the
buoyant upholding of God's constant action in our existence. "Seek first [God's] kingdom and his righteousness,
and all these [other] things shall be yours as well."[44]

It would appear, then, that the validity of the humanist
ethic depends, not so much upon the adequacy of their
description of what man's good would be, but upon the
truth of their denial of the reality and primacy of God's
providence and grace in human life. For if God exists at
all, He is the ground and final referent of man's ethical values as truly as He is of the creative process in which these
values are known and actualized. If God exists, as the Christians profess to know Him, the shape and ordering of man's

true good is to be measured by His design for human fulfillment. And the inmost energy which transforms man's
motives and loyalties comes from His love and grace as they
are responded to, in trustful reliance, by faithful men. The
humanist can make nothing of this, since it clearly over-
rides the first article of his religious faith: viz., "I believe
in man, maker of the image of God as the symbol of man's
power." The Christian wisdom, for its part, both in its ethical and theological enterprise rests on and derives from the
Christian faith in God, who has given us a valid and effica-
cious self-presentation in Jesus Christ. It is only thus that
we can rightly relate life's lived-out goods and meaning to
the first and final reality of our existence.

The Christian readily agrees with the psychotherapist
about the supremacy of love among the virtues and the
power of true love to order life to its true and highest possibilities. But the Christian cannot find the source and sanction of such love in nature or society, however generously
construed. Passion there is, and the dark strugglings of eros:
now in Dionysiac revel, now in Orphic ecstasy. And logos
there is, and the power of mind to order and direct the natural energies of the world. Passion and reason may be fused:
passion disciplined by reason and reason vitalized by passion—and this creates the highest level of secular civilization and culture. But the love which called us into being,
and orders us to our proper ends, comes from above and
beyond nature, above and beyond our possessing or manipulation. It is a love which flows out of ultimate plenitude;
it does not arise from depletion and need. It is a love which

can rightly secure and guarantee the true worth and value of the human person, since it is the chief motive for his creation. It is the love of God. This, for the Christian, is the true source of the human love which purifies and transforms, which brings harmony and health into our disorder.[45]

Man can no more generate true love by his own powers than he can have generated his own true being. Love is the grace of true being. It comes to us as a gift, just as life itself. But all our gifts, accepted in responsible freedom, become projects and tasks for us in their use. Thus, "in this is love, not that we loved God but that he loved us. . . . Beloved, if God so loved us, we also ought to love one another."[46] Human love remains forever human, is forever set within the boundaries of finite existence. Human love which is not response to divine love is, therefore, a self-referring, self-interested love which enlightenment can direct but not transform. But the denial of the transcendence of human love by God's love is, finally, a denial of self-transcendence—since the only authentic power by which the self can be lifted above and beyond the natural order in which it emerges is God's creative grace which invests His human creatures with the glory of the infinite.

The defect of an ethic of self-affirmation is, ironically enough, that it fails to affirm the human self sufficiently, in its widest dimensions and outreach. It can, indeed, serve as a useful support for the concepts of human dignity and self-respect (especially in the face of other secular schemes which despise and brutalize man). It can guide the moral judgment in its struggle to control the impersonal energies of human life. But the finite self, thus self-affirmed, is still no more than another item in a natural process which remains impersonal. Thus, personal values are derived from an impersonal ground. The personal values are then affirmed to be higher than the process in which they emerge. But this is difficult either to understand or to believe. Man cannot, by and for himself, affirm his own true worth. Only his Creator can do that. It is God who affirms us rightly. It is in His love for us that we can find and accept our true evaluation and self-estimate. But this means self-denial of the polar self-sufficiency of our own existence.

The Christian teaching of self-denial as the way to life's best ordering is easily misconstrued by the non-Christian as a self-directed assault upon the self. It is also easily distorted in practice by the nominal Christian (whose masochistic tendencies have another history) as a deliberate program for meriting salvation. But this is only another neurotic stratagem which seeks to win by weakness what it could not gain by naked force. On the other hand, the Christian who denies his polar and prime value in the world finds, unaccountably, a new basis of self-estimate: viz., God's affirmation of him, as an object of divine care and love, and therefore a person of sacred worth and meaning. The Christian loves himself *propter Deum*, because, and in terms, of God's love for him. "He loves himself, takes care of himself, performs duties to himself, and endeavors to acquire strength of character in himself, all as a part of Christian vocation bending his energies to other people's necessities."[47]

In such an ethic, a man may come to self-knowledge and self-acceptance because he is known and accepted—and affirmed—by the selfsame God who made him and who was in Christ reconciling the world—and we with it—unto Himself. The Christian's self-estimate, therefore, is curiously independent of the appraisals of the world. His "justification" does not rest with others nor even with himself; this reduces a fruitful source of anxiety. He knows himself as well-beloved and reconciled—and this from God, who sets a task with every blessing. God's *agape* imparts new moral power to the faithful man. It humanizes passion without destroying it. It suffuses the intellect with the warmth of goodness which lights the way to truth.

The Christian ethic of obedient love can readily find room and welcome for the practical import and humane ideals of the psychological ethic—but only if there is a prior acknowledgment that the reason and love on which the psychotherapist relies is measured by the mind and heart of God. Given such a commitment, the Christian ethic joins in firm emphasis upon self-control and on the *ordinate* satisfactions of human needs, for the intelligent upbuilding of those forms of social life which make for freedom and community. By the same authority it stands against man's abuse of his freedom and the inhumanity which flows from it. It calls for justice, not as an abstract calculation of rights, but as a constant and personal concern for the neighbor's well-doing and well-being. It demands a constant vigilance against the violation or deprivation of human rights and goods, by whomsoever they may be threatened. It stands against all absolutizing of relative values, that is, against all idolatry—since God alone is final judge of worth and value in His creation. When Christians have been truly obedient in their love of God, they have had an important share in God's leveling of the arrogant and in His breaking down the walls of partition between class and race and national pride systems.[48]

The Christian ethic grounds the dignity of man in his double relation to God and neighbor. Valid self-respect grows from man's assurance of God's righteous love and concern for all men and their worth. But with *dignity*, in the Christian way, there also goes *humility*, which is a very different thing from self-contempt. The humble Christian is not one who cringes before God or his fellow humans— or heaps contumely upon his own head in the hope of blunting the force of God's wrath and man's scorn. Rather, he is a person who knows himself accepted of God; he has come to rely on God's love and grace as the power of his life. He is, therefore, quite past the "humiliations" which the frustrations of finite existence bring to self-sufficing pride. Because he is beloved and because the love is from his Creator and Redeemer, he can overcome his sense of basic insecurity and rise above his elemental fears of rejection and extinction. Thus, sacrificial service to others becomes possible without the corrosive feelings of self-righteousness or self-pity.

At yet another crucial point, the Christian ethic and the humanist ethic of psychotherapy stand in fundamental conflict. This is the problem of the management and repair of wrongdoing, error and sin. For the humanist ethic, this is primarily a human affair. As men achieve insight into their own motives and those of others, they find it more and more possible to discard their feelings of guilt and condemnation, and to forgive themselves and others. "To understand all is to forgive all." There is, obviously, much neurotic guilt and morbid condemnation which arises from pejorative attitudes toward self and others which can, and ought to be, handled by the psychological process of self-examination and acquittal. Human errors may be identified as such—and dealt with constructively in a permissive situation where reason and love prevail. But the humanist appears to contend that this is *all* there is to the problem of human wrongdoing and its repair.

Yet even the psychological mechanisms of guilt and self-condemnation are clues to the transcendental character of man's conflict with his "conscience." To grant the general thesis that the standard stuff of conscience is a montage of social judgments still does not dispose of the question of the wider outreach of moral judgment. There is a dimension in human wrongdoing which far exceeds ignorance and miscalculation. It is unfaith, irresponsibility, sin—and its bitter fruit is estrangement and separation from God *and* neighbor. And even when unacknowledged and repressed this miscarriage of existence continues to disturb and demoralize the minds and hearts of men. Man never sins against himself alone—nor only against his neighbor and humanity. He sins against God—and for this he cannot forgive himself, nor be absolved by any other man. If man is to be reconciled to God—and to his fellows and his own true self—his sins must be dealt with, without indulgence and without loss of real humanity. They must be *forgiven* by God.

Forgiveness is, therefore, a central issue for any ethic—and for any concept of psychic health. And if one recognizes that self-forgiveness is inadequate, the problem remains as to how a man may find God's forgiveness and enter into the self-acceptance which comes from God's loving acceptance of us. Two popular, but false, ways may be quickly noticed. One is the idea that forgiveness may be earned, or merited, or wrung from a cosmic martinet—by self-punishment, or expiatory sacrifice, preferably substitutionary. This is, indeed, the heresy which begets most of the unhealthy symptoms of morbid guilt and sado-masochism which we can see associated with neurotic religiousness. But there is an opposite distortion of the truth: the complacent assurance that forgiveness is automatically provided by a God of love. It is hard to know how sincere or how satirical Heine was in his famous crack about forgiveness: *Le bon Dieu pardonerra mes pèchés, c'est son métier.* But there can be no doubt that there are many people in our churches who subscribe to a highly sentimental and self-indulgent version of this same doctrine—and so miss the force of the Christian prophetic demand for the remaking of life under God's righteous rule.

The Christian experience of forgiveness is not an earned acquittal nor an indulgent dismissal of the guilty. It is not, primarily, a forensic affair at all. Man, repentant, faces the transforming reordering impact of God's grace on man's disorder. The "moral law" is neither relaxed nor violated. God's righteousness is not annulled. Man is made aware of God's demand that "all righteousness be fulfilled." He comes to know that God's love has made cost to Himself in reconciling His estranged but beloved children to Himself. The distinction between sin and the sinner is firmly maintained. Thus the Christian man forgiven can cast away the guilt and shame of his sins without a self-indulgent sense of complacency. One of the most striking aspects of the Christian teaching about forgiveness is that "he who would be forgiven must himself forgive."[49] Thus the way of reconciliation to God is never unilateral; it always reaches out toward neighbor and community.

It is unfortunate that neither Christian ethical theorists nor the psychotherapists have paid enough attention to the medieval distinction between remorse (*attritio*) and contrition (*contritio*), in the human response to acknowledged wrongdoing. "Attrition" is the self-directed verdict of guilty —with or without mercy. It is, of course, a form of self-punishment. No wonder, then, that it does great psychological harm and little or no religious good. Christian contrition, true repentance, is the honest owning of the wrong, and the free acceptance of responsibility—both in the atmosphere of God's redeeming love as we know it in Christ Jesus. It means more than self-rebuke; it means accepting God's just judgment of our unfaith. It means far more than an easy rescue; it is the frank confession of our reliance on

God's grace as the authentic power in our reconciliation to God and our recovery of moral insight and energy.

Because the Christian believes that God's righteousness is loving, and His love righteous, he rests assured of the eternal verity of righteousness and love. Because he has experienced forgiveness neither cheap nor magical, he finds a new power of self-commitment in ethical enterprise. Because he knows God's love as ungrudging and redemptive, the care for code-keeping drops away. He might even teach the psychotherapists a thing or two about the overthrow of the superego and the overscrupulous conscience. Paul's claim that "where sin increased, grace abounded all the more"[50] expresses the paradox of Christian sensitivity to sin and confidence in God's mercy. When Luther exhorted the timid, staid Melancthon "to sin bravely," he was hacking away, in his typical heavy-handed fashion, at the futility of the puritanic effort to hold one's sinning down to a forgivable minimum—since it is the quality of *repentance* that avails for forgiveness and not the balanced budget of one's sins. And if it is God's grace which undermines the tyranny of our superego, then we are free indeed!

The Christian ordering of life aims at the same goals as that of the highest vision of the psychological ethic: reason, love, spontaneity and emancipation from the slaveries of self and society. The basic motif of the Christian ethic is *responsible love*. It is, therefore, "ego-syntonic" since all significant ethical decisions spring from the human self in its state of knowing and being known of God: this is the self at its freest and most authentic self-affirmation. The results of such ethical motivation show themselves in devoted and responsible service to the neighbor and society. But *all* the human virtues are "fruits," by-products of the primary and basic reality in Christian living: communion with God and the life of grace in which this is concretely realized in worship, service and the deeds of love and community.

The ethical judgments of Christians are, inevitably, relativistic and fallible.[51] But God's righteous rule, to which our relativistic judgments refer, is apodictic and nonrelative. God's demand for righteousness, faith and love stands beyond man's power to obey forthwith—and yet the demand remains as the norm and measure of the relative approximations of it that men achieve. The Christian criticism of society is, therefore, not ameliorative (though it seeks and welcomes every realistic "improvement" in a given situation). It is, in principle, a revolutionary ethic which seeks a radical change in the inner motives and hopes of men-in-society. Because of this radical demand, all human achievements must be judged in the eschatological light of God's kingdom and final purposes. There is no Christian blueprint for the perfect state or economic order, but there is the Christian requirement that political forms be valued only as instruments for the free association of responsible men in a devoted community—or that an economic order be judged by the measure of its service to the legitimate economic needs of *all* the people. In the Christian ordering of life, the place of privilege is that of service and fellowship

—all other forms of caste and hierarchy are condemned. And for the primal energy which moves the heart and will of faith to good works, the Christian's sole dependence is upon the grace of God.

In the area of ethics, as well as elsewhere, the Christian can well afford to welcome and appropriate the new insights and emphases of psychotherapy. Especially in its analysis of self-control and the primacy of love, psychotherapy has greatly added to our understanding of the correlation between mental health and moral virtue—and has ranged itself alongside the Christian cause of responsible freedom in ethical decision, against all heteronomous codes and legalism. But the Christian ethical teacher must conclude that the psychological ethic thus far developed by psychotherapy is generally secularized and autonomous and, insofar as this is the case, it is incompatible with the Christian conception of the *theonomous* ordering of life. He must also judge that, for all its realism, the psychological ethic is superficial in its estimate of the weight of sin and the malignancy of polar self-love. Its concept of love, though noble and releasing in comparison with the strictures of petty and conventional morality, is still that of human eros. It is thus a notion which denies man's need of God's *agape* by the really desperate expedient of denying the reality of God.

Thus the Christian will ask the psychotherapists that they explore yet once again, and further, the assumptions of their analysis of the moral life. They must either buttress and make explicit their naturalistic religion and their humanist ethic, by frank appeals to the grounds of their basic faith and tested religious knowledge; or else, they must be willing to consider the real option of the Christian message as an ample context for all the positive values of the psychological ethic and the valid extension of the human quest for good which must fail unless it finds the grace of God as the seeking love which leads all human quest to its goals.

Only the self-respect given in self-denial; only the self-control gained from God's guidance of the human will; only the freedom liberated in repentance and trust; only the knowledge which grows in the course of Christian discipleship and cross-bearing; only the goodness generated by grace—only in these good gifts which God gives freely to His children can man find his true order and blessedness. Only by these virtues growing in the soul can man order his life according to God's design. Only in the life of grace is reason redeemed and eros transformed into the vital synthesis of all human energy and capacity.

The demoralization of modern civilization is profound and it threatens us with unimaginable disaster. Man's destructiveness and inhumanity gain more powerful weapons and a wider scope. As human idealism and the moral effects of modern communication affect the hopes and fears of men, we see a disturbing paradox. Men and nations have a yearning for peace and prosperity which is at least more articulate than ever before and yet the endless turmoil in the affairs of the nations and among them is so frustrating of men's hopes that cynicism and despair rise and spread like a noxious fog among large segments and groups of modern society. In the time of their greatest achievements, reason and liberty stand in deadly peril.

In an age of unreason, high religion has every right and duty to make common cause with all the curative and redemptive forces at work in human society. And of these, as we have seen in many ways, psychotherapy is surely one of the most significant. But in the alliance with psychotherapy, Christians must still point to the context in which, as they believe, the best therapy can be conceived and practiced. This is the "dynamic field" of Christian faith and devotion, in which man finds the courage by which to live and to die in the love of God, who shunned not self-sacrifice in order to deliver us "from . . . the dominion of darkness and transferred us to the kingdom of his beloved Son, in whom we have redemption, the forgiveness of sins."[52]

CHAPTER SIX

The Terms of the Alliance

We have now explored, in synoptic fashion, four of
the basic human concerns in which psychotherapy and
Christian thought have a common stake. No attempt has
been made to survey any single area exhaustively and many
points of interest and importance have been omitted—
some by design, others inadvertently. A detailed account of
the entire range of psychotherapeutic theory and Christian
doctrine lies quite beyond the scope of our present purpose
—and competence. It is enough if we have succeeded in
drawing to a convergent focus the main lines of interpretation in both fields and if we have made plain the essential
distinctions between their basic *modes* of interpretation.

In every area thus explored, we have discovered a significantly stable pattern of agreement and disagreement. In
point of practical wisdom, and in the middle axioms, the
agreements between modern psychotherapy and contemporary Christianity are very considerable and mutually re-
enforcing. Christianity needs, and can readily appropriate,
not only the clinical aid afforded by the psychotherapists
themselves but also the critique and correction of much

that passes for Christian worship, teaching and conduct which is, in fact, derived from outmoded concepts of psychology and the unhealthy residues of substandard ethical and theological notions. The alliance between psychotherapy and Christianity, therefore, offers many practical advantages to the Christian care of souls and not a few to a fully humane and effectual psychotherapy.

But the disagreements which have also appeared in our analysis run very deep; indeed, they serve to vitiate or undermine a real and honest alliance. We have identified, I think, a serious clash in primitive assumptions which divides the general movement of psychotherapy from the main traditions of historic Christianity. It is a conflict of basic truth claims respecting basic faiths, a disjunction between world views and first principles. The general import of modern psychotherapy involves a serious denial of the essential truth claims of the Christian doctrines of nature, man and God, and the assertion (if only by implication) of a full budget of contrary premises. The vast majority of psychotherapists regard historic Christianity as an obsolescent mode of interpreting human problems which is now in process of being superseded by the superior wisdom of the new sciences of man, among which psychotherapy stands chief. The Christian cure of souls is to be judged by the criteria of scientific psychology—and the round of its assertions which cannot be thus validated must be discredited and discarded. Much of the incidental wisdom of Christianity, acquired by its trial-and-error experiences in history, is still allowable. Moreover, in an age not yet fully hospitable to the hegemony of science in human affairs, religion has its continuing significant uses for morale-building, for social sanctions and controls. But the truth claims of high religion are illusory, since they cannot be derived from scientific truth and they contradict what is widely assumed to be the scientific world view. Psychotherapy, on the other hand, rests and builds on the sure foundations of science and is able to push forward its frontiers of wisdom by the self-consistent methods of scientific knowledge.

To many Christians, this pejorative estimate of their faith threatens mortal danger, which can only be countered with stern denial and the vigorous assertion of the dogmatic claims of the Christian message. Even to argue with a psychotherapist who reduces Christian proclamation to "psychological material" is to weaken the Christian position. It is, as Barth has charged, to treat the unfaith of the pagan seriously. But this is, in effect, to give up hope for a productive alliance between psychotherapy and Christianity. It would also tend to freeze the traditional *cura animarium* where it was before the advent of depth psychology. It is, moreover, equivalent to reasserting the omnicompetence of religion in direct antithesis to the rival claims of science. This is, surely, a desperate expedient—and quite unnecessary. If it should turn out that psychotherapy is by no means as formidable as it seems to be in its evocation of the authority of science as the sanction of its faith, Christians might then find for themselves a new freedom for their own critical enterprise—of inspecting the world's wisdom in the full confidence that no valid scientific knowledge can overthrow the basic Christian faith in God as Creator, Redeemer and Consummator—and in the world as the dynamic field of "God's grace and man's hope."

The alliance we are here proposing between the practical wisdom of psychotherapy and the Christian wisdom about life and destiny is, I believe, quite feasible. It would represent the authentic wisdoms which each affords and sidetrack the borrowed wisdoms which each requires for its completion. Psychotherapy's practical wisdom is its very own, empirically founded. The naturalistic world view it generally exhibits is *borrowed*. Christianity's *practical wisdom* is largely borrowed; its theistic world view is its very own, the bone and marrow of its Gospel. A psychotherapy which freely admitted the Christian doctrines of God and men as the referential "frame" of its empirical work could be well consorted with a Christian care of souls which fully acknowledge the direction and counsel of scientific psychotherapy.

Christianity has never been able to rest its basic claims to truth upon the authority of science. It has no specific "science" of its own and has been constantly forced to appropriate and adjust to the scientific wisdom of the surrounding intellectual milieu. This has been the case even with Christians who are piously oblivious of the sources of their picture of nature and the world. What is worse, Christians have often gotten so attached to certain borrowed scientific items that they have taken them up into the faith itself, so that when the old science is superseded by later developments, the faith itself suffers the charge of being as outmoded as the scientific notions with which it had become so closely associated in the minds—and faith—of the people. A familiar and prime example of this is the close association of medieval theology and Ptolemaic astronomy. The Christians taught, as a prime article of faith, that God is real and perfect being. The Ptolemaic model of the planetary system was based on the Greek assumption that the circle and circular motion represent the highest degree of geometrical perfection. A universe in which the earth is the center and the planets move in complex circles (cycles and epicycles) was readily understood as just the sort of world a perfect Creator might have been expected to make. Galilei's denial of the geocentric system and his broad claim that "the laws of motion are the laws of all things" seemed to strike at Christian faith itself. Kepler's brilliant hypothesis that the model for planetary motion is not the circle but the ellipse opened the way for the new astronomy and physics to develop, but it was also a major blow at the popular concepts of theism, in which men had confused their knowledge of God with their empirical knowledge of mass in motion. In every age of decisive scientific progress, or reformulation, Christianity has felt the shock in its own fabric—and always because its concern for conserving the unchanging truth outreaches itself to try to cover the truth that was made for changing. Christianity exists, therefore, in uneasy tension with the ongoing evolution of science. It is often charged that one of Christianity's main interests is to dominate and control scientific inquiry; and there are ex·ceptional instances where this was—and still may be—a deliberate purpose. But far more normally, Christianity's motive in its dealings with science has been to maintain the scientific notions to which it has already managed to adjust and from which the threat of religious rivalry has finally been removed!

The thoughtful Christian has no reasonable ground of anxiety about science in its analysis and description of the events and processes in the world. He has no just complaint against the hypothetical, or controlling, knowledge which science yields for the human mastery and use of nature. But there is real substance to the Christian fear that the scientist who thus succeeds in describing or controlling natural process will thereupon overreach the limitations of his scientific method and claim that "what is not science is not knowledge"! The Christian faith can assimilate any scientific claim save one: the claim that the omnicompetence of science is scientifically verifiable. For this is equivalent to the claim that human knowledge is self-validating—and to the denial of the necessity and relevance of revelation as the ground for human insight into ultimate truth.

There is the familiar story of Napoleon and P. S. Laplace, the French astronomer, whose nebular hypothesis was a sort of evolutionary theory of the development of our solar system—and who was an implacable foe of any theistic world view. Napoleon is reported to have commented: "They tell me, Monsieur Laplace, that you have written a great book on the system of the world and have never even mentioned God as its Creator." "No, sire," replied Laplace, "I had no need of such an hypothesis. It is superfluous!"

There is, of course, a sober truth in this rejoinder. There *is* no need of God, as immanent agent, in any astronomical theory. Cosmology can do its work without necessary reference to God. But we further know that M. Laplace, and many of his mechanistic colleagues, believed, with soaring exultation, that if God is not needed to *describe* the world, He can therewith be *dismissed* from the world as a superfluity. For the reductive naturalist, it is but a few steps from a description of the world which does not refer to God, to a description of a godless world—having no need of God to explain, or be referent for, anything at all! Where God is not required for a descriptive hypothesis, He may be omitted from all consideration whatsoever. And what then —what remains? Science, omnicompetent science, which offers men a world view, an ethic and a gospel—with God exiled from it all by the law of parsimony!

Something like this has accompanied the evolution of modern psychotherapy. In *The Future of an Illusion*, Freud explained the psychological mechanisms of religious projections and showed that the popular role assigned to God in religion is based upon "illusion"—i.e., a conception which can be neither proved nor disproved by science. Since His reality and relevance cannot be settled by the only means Freud believed appropriate for human knowledge, such ideas can be branded as *illusion*, superfluous notions destined to wither away as science expands and occupies the terrain they once shrouded in their mist. *"Science is no illusion. But it would be an illusion to suppose that we could get anywhere else what it cannot give us.*"[1] Laplace, *redivivus!!*

And we have seen that the psychotherapists, both near to and far from Freud's clinical doctrine, have followed him here. Fromm, Flugel and their company assume the non-reality of God with as little attention to the critical warrant for their denial as when the average pious Christian assumes their assertions. And, if you can assume the non-reality of God, it is directly consistent to proceed to interpret the data of religious experience as having *psychological* importance but no metaphysical basis.

Psychotherapy has thus shared in the familiar, and tragic, process by which modern science has helped to dispossess the traditional theism of its ancient holdings and has laid the foundation for the new forms secularist and humanist faiths to build upon.

This is the process quite familiar by now in the evolution of modern science. As each new science has emerged, it has challenged the notions and correlations of the older sciences. The fact that Christianity may have made its peace, and some sort of alliance with the older sciences, is now used to discredit Christianity as archaic. First, it was the new astronomy, physics and chemistry. Christianity had barely adjusted to the revolutionary import of their theories when the new biology threw the situation into a fresh confusion. Now, after Christian thought has managed to assimilate the Darwinian wisdom in terms which are, or can be, compatible with the Christian faith, the new psychology comes forth to upset the achieved stability between Christianity and the older sciences. And, in every circling round of this process, man remains—and, most of all, scientific man—to claim that he is the measure and the measurer of all knowledge and value.

Modern psychotherapy has followed this cycle—but within the inner temple of human self-concern. In its explorations, it has found no heuristic necessity for the idea of God, for the concept of the self as finite substance, nor for the objective order of right and good. From this, it has tended to conclude that an adequate account of human existence, and all our real concerns, can now be given without any further notice to the ancient claims of Christian truth on these points. Thus, despite important but infrequent exceptions, modern psychotherapists, in large majority, regard the naturalistic world view in which they work as scientifically valid—as much so as the clinical methods by which they work. It is the current end product of that tendency in modern science which began with Galilei's broad claim that "the laws of motion are the laws of all things" and is now expressed in Fromm's gospel of "man for himself."

Now, the ironic twist to this immense ideological development of modern times is that it rests upon a gigantic *non sequitur*. It simply does not follow from the fact that scientific description can dispense with God as immanent agent that the reality and relevance of God in nature and human existence are thereby disproved! Nothing in modern science, as such, requires or even supports atheism or naturalism as a world any more than it requires or supports theism.[2]

The various forms of naturalism and humanism which we have seen associated with psychotherapy-turned-philosophy are grounded in "primitive" assumptions which cannot be "proved" or "disproved" by the scientific methods used in clinic and analytic theory. The claim that these assumptions are the only ones fully compatible with the practical wisdom of psychotherapy is a curious instance of the plainly unscientific fallacy of composition. Reductive naturalism is a basic faith. Christian theism is a basic faith. Neither can displace the other by authoritarian appeals to science—whether it be the old science with which Christianity had made a partial peace or the new science which fancies itself strong enough to walk through the world alone.

If the truth of naturalism cannot be verified by the science which espouses it, and thus vanquish all rivals by the authority of science, it is still a significant belief and ought to be appraised on other grounds—along with all other significant beliefs. The first questions to be asked of a basic, but "nonverifiable" belief are, What psychodynamic role does it play in the existence of the believer? What is the psychic gain derived from it?

It is a clear impression which grows as I have surveyed the ethical and philosophical ideas of the psychotherapists under review, that their basic faith in naturalism has something in it of a *security operation*. Their charge that religious faith in God is a projection of infantile wishes upon the cosmos is not wholly free from its own projective aspects. If, as a Christian, I *want* God to be, is it possible that another man, a naturalist, *does not want* God to be? The dismissal of God by the naturalists and humanists—or His redefinition so that He becomes either part or the sum of nature—is no sad bereavement! If religious faith reflects an infantile regression, so naturalistic faith looks a good deal like the adolescent rejection of the father, as a precondition to self-assertion. "God is dead!" "Perhaps man can now rise ever higher from the time when he no longer flows away into a God!"[3] The psychodynamic function of this kind of naturalism is, as it seems to me, man's invocation of nature and man's highest form of "controlled knowledge" (science) in behalf of man's own hegemony and autarchy in existence.

Of course, the same question must be asked about the Christian belief in God as the world's creator and the ground and end of human existence. What is *its* psychodynamic function? Here the answers are numerous and familiar: the father-protector, the heavenly compensation for earthly deprivations. There is a heavy layer of truth in this, as we have seen. But, when we clear away the bad science and neurotic religion which have overlaid historic Christianity, there is still a basic dynamic function of such a faith which can be discovered, even by the nonparticipating observer. The Christian faith seeks and finds the meaning of life and the worth of human existence in being itself, in being beyond nature and existence, in the one, only, living God, in whom we live and move and have our being. Christian faith begins with man's inescapable, radical dependence and finds its rest in nothing less than the utterly dependable, the truly sufficient reality which establishes all our hopes and love securely.

And if we thus compare these two basic beliefs in their respective psychodynamic functions, we can see more clearly the ground of our choice between them. For choose we must—and a suspended judgment finally falls toward the claim for man's supremacy since it is he who has the power of choosing to decline to choose. Naturalism is man's declaration of independence and sovereignty in the world which he measures and values for himself. Theism is man's acknowledgment of radical dependence upon God and his finitely-free responsibility as creature and citizen of God's beloved community. Naturalism stands for man's freedom-in-autarchy; theism for freedom-in-dependence. Naturalism stands for human values specified by human valuations; theism for human values specified by God's righteous will. Naturalism stands for love as the highest human virtue; theism for love as God's greatest gift to man and His highest will for man. How shall we choose between them?

It is easy for Christians to blame the naturalists for many of the world's tragic burdens of woe and grief—for much of which they are themselves grimly responsible. And yet is it possible to deny that as men have absorbed, by knowledge or opinion, the secularistic world views of naturalism and humanism, they have lost by so much, a positive faith in human existence, its transcendent meaning and worth? Is it not a plain fact that modern man, in his art, his literature, his aesthetic visions of himself and his economic and political experiments in human community—this man, who rejects God and declares himself supreme, has, in fact, devalued himself and his fellows?[4] It may be that modern atheisms of all the different sorts seek a new and higher meaning for life beyond the ruins of the wishful fantasies of a religious world view. But the effect thus far, in three centuries of militant secularism, is modern man's disenchantment, despair and mass demoralization. Man's secularized devotion to "humanity" has not turned out to be more actually humane than his old-fashioned sinful inhumanity to man.

Naturalism is a basic faith. It has its articles of belief, its credo.[5] The first article is, of course, the denial of God and the assertion that the world is governed by impersonal physical forces (gravitation, electricity, physical and chemical process). From this it follows that the world or nature is the sum or total of everything there is. This world has no purpose or meaning in itself—save to be as it is. It has no moral order and lays no imperatives on its "creatures"—save that they come to be and pass away after their kind. But man, within this impersonal order, has his own values and purposes and from them produces a moral and social order, subjective and human. There is no categorical imperative for there is no source or ground for any such thing. Man can seek or hope for no guidance or justification in the world or beyond it. For, if God is not, man is, and must be, the master of his fate, the captain of his soul.[6]

If all our knowledge and all our wisdom *required* this view of us, we should be forced by "the long courage of the truth" to accept and maintain it, even in the curious paradox of confidence and despair which come from a humanist faith. It would, indeed, give us confidence in ourselves and our human enterprise, fortified and guided by the strong hand of scientific method. But the confidence from such a faith turns into despair when the human enterprise falls afoul of catastrophe and repeated frustration of utopian hopes. Indeed, we can see everywhere around us even now the signs of profound demoralization and the desolation of the spirit of modern man.[7]

Fortunately, no such faith is required of us or anyone— and the invocation of the magisterial authority of science is an illicit appeal of false simplicity. The Christian faith is at least an equal option for the thoughtful man who stands in the crisis of commitment. It is at least as intelligible a faith, resting on at least as much experiential evidence and exhibiting a capacity to interpret the inescapable issues of human life in a fashion both more meaningful and truly profound. The truth claims of the Christian faith cannot be "proved" —any more than those of the humanist. But they can be tested, by those who place themselves inside the circle of faith—tested by the criteria of truth and righteousness, tested by the self-validating experiences of high communion with God and common life in the Christian fellowship. Moreover, the Christian faith can be an ample and hospitable context for the scientific enterprise, in all its proper dimensions and concerns.

In the Christian view of being, nature is not and cannot be self-intelligible nor self-contained. Nature is the totality of the causal order, as wide and far as it may reach. But there is always a "beyondness" in every reference to nature and this bears a close relation to the degree of *personal* action involved. Freedom, sin, grace and goodness all point past the round of natural process and order to what Kant called "a pure intelligible world," the thought, will and purpose of God Himself.

> The multitude of interwoven adaptations by which the world is constituted a theatre of life, intelligence and morality, cannot reasonably be regarded as an outcome of mechanism, or of blind formative power, or of aught but purposive intelligence.[8]

There is a radical cleavage between any view of the universe which regards it as being in itself, and a view of the universe as grounded in being beyond the world.[9] The former comes finally to deify nature; the latter affirms the primacy of God as Creator and Sustainer of all existence, for whom freedom, spirit and love are the links which bind all creative and created wisdoms together into a single system of truth and goodness. There is an impressive case to be made out for the basic contention that the round of process and reality, as we know it, can best be understood as the creation of ultimate Power and Love rather than as a self-contained or self-referable entity. This is simply said in the Christian affirmation of faith in the Living God, who is "maker of heaven and earth and of all things visible and invisible."[10]

There can be no honest and productive alliance between the Christian and the humanist world views. Their differences cannot be composed by minor concessions from either side. If modern psychotherapy is inextricably bound to the humanism of its major spokesmen, there must then be a final rivalry between the evangel of man's sufficiency and the evangel of God's grace. But this, too, is by no means necessary and very far from the desirable or right solution to our problem.

Christianity has neither the right, nor the power, to displace or eliminate the reigning naturalism in psychotherapy by fiat or decree. It has no right—and, I should hope, no desire—to foster a rival psychotherapy which is merely tailored to fit the dogmas and traditions of historic Christianity.[11] But Christianity has the right and the duty to analyze and evaluate the terms of its alliance with any empiric discipline, and to examine the *de facto* outlook of the operatives in a given field. It has the right to ask of psychotherapy that its prevailing presuppositions be reviewed at a new level of self-critical inquiry. It has the right to hope that a psychotherapy truly open to and compatible with high religion might come to be developed and the dominance of the now reigning secularism might be broken.

The fruitful collaboration of psychotherapy and the Christian enterprise will involve important re-evaluations in the "traditional" patterns of exposition and self-understanding. A psychotherapy which *intends* to ally itself with the Christian care of souls must "make room" for such concepts as those of a discrete and responsible selfhood, of human sin more tragic than error, of grace more effectual than nature or fortune. It must, in short, make place for God—

and for a wisdom about life which draws a circle wider than description and draws its truth from a deeper well than science. It must acknowledge the propriety of *revelation* and *faith* as modes of valid wisdom—not heuristic substitutes for scientific inquiry but as the vital fonts from which come the clues and commitments which launch and guide our reasonings.

Christian thought, for its part, if it expects to appropriate the practical wisdom of psychotherapy must likewise "make room" for some basic ideas which *are* integral to the clinical practice of good psychotherapy. The first of these is *eros*, human love and vitality. Christians have often been uneasy, or downright confused, about the relation of human and divine love—and have too readily disparaged the goodness and positive meaning of man's erotic life. Much neurotic shame and guilt have come from a false embarrassment with the natural processes of our physical existence—and a false disjunction between the upward aspirations of human love and the redemptive outreach of God's love and grace. Psychotherapy has done much to teach us the rightness of the natural—and Christianity must needs acknowledge the value of this basic truth and draw the appropriate conclusions for morals.

Moreover, any Christian teaching in mutual alliance with psychotherapy must make room for the psychotherapeutic emphasis upon *logos*—the search for rational patterns even in human misbehavior and disorder. This means a careful and deep-running distinction between neurosis and sin; between the human distortions which can be remedied by the powers of human wisdom and love and the estrangement-in-being which can be remedied only by God's reconciling grace. The universality of logos-in-life and the divine source and identity of all truth wherever it appears —this is not a strange or inadmissible concept for Christians and it is indispensable for any effective and mutual tie with any human wisdom which must rely on rational inquiry as the guide to truth.

Finally, Christian doctrine, if it is to share in common work with modern psychotherapy must make an ungrudging place for a concept of IUSTITIA *originalis* as well as PECCATUM *originalis*. It is a firm tenet of biblical faith that God's creation is good—insofar as it is and remains within the pattern of the divine intent. Man has undoubtedly marred and disfigured the *imago dei* in his inmost nature. But man's essential being has neither been destroyed by sin, nor can it be—since God is not powerless to hold in being that which He created in love. Nor is man without a residue of this "original righteousness" even in his presently disordered life. He is not without a viable germ of justice in his selfhood, for otherwise the work of redemptive grace would be incongruous for the task of remaking human nature after God's *original* design. Humanism has clearly made too much of man's indefectible goodness, yet, on the other hand, *some* versions of Christianity have come perilously close to teaching that the original sin is being a man at all! But psychotherapy's demonstration—for it amounts to that —of the nisus to health in human nature, and the residues of virtue which open the way to active righteousness, must be taken seriously by any Christian ethic and soteriology which is honestly concerned to acknowledge and use the resources of the modern arts of healing. After a century of rather fatuous liberal optimism about human goodness, followed by the recent quarter-century of disenchantment and downward revision of our estimates of human virtue, the time is past due for a Christian doctrine of man which holds in solid balance both classical motifs of original sin *and* original righteousness—to the end that we may honestly account for the virtues which psychotherapy discovers in the human maturation and also for the radical need for conversion, faith and grace which carry us far beyond the resources of human therapy.

Christianity has survived many an eager requiem composed by the confident pagans. For all its manifest defects it is, one might well believe, here to stay. Psychotherapy, for its part, is likewise a staple element in modern life. It would be a senseless, tragic thing if these two vital enterprises stood off as rivals or wrestled for a single uncontested crown. The alliance we have been recommending in this book is not only a live possibility. It is one of the most urgent opportunities before either psychotherapy or Christianity. Each may claim its own sufficiency. There is plausible—and disastrous—precedent for this. Psychotherapy can continue in the humanist faith of its childhood and adolescence and become the false religion of a true science. Christianity can borrow its psychology from other sources —and become a true religion of a false science. Either of these miscarriages would miss the obvious way between:

that psychotherapy make room in its *practical* wisdom for the *first principles* of the Christian message and that Christianity, for its part, should make an ample place in its wisdom-about-life for the clinical truth and effective service proffered by psychotherapy. Anything less than this would entail a serious loss to the truth of psychotherapy and to the efficacy of the Christian care of souls.

What is called for—and what seems to me clearly possible—is a *division of labor*, on the one hand, and *a synthesis of goals*, on the other. The professional therapist cannot do the work of the Christian minister, nor can the minister replace the therapist. But both could do their proper work with the same assumptions and goals derived from a basic Christian faith and commitment. The time is fully ripe for those psychotherapists who are devout believers in God— there are a few, and in good standing, too—to undertake the exploration of the issues in their field in the light of their faith. The believing physician must show that his science concretes his faith as his faith supplies ultimate meaning to his science. And on the other side, the well-furnished Christian minister must enlist in the arduous enterprise of really learning from the psychotherapists—and appropriating all possible aid from them in understanding himself and his task more adequately. Together, in joint projects, the believing physician and the well-furnished minister may widen and enrich their service to God and their fellows far beyond what we have known from either in the past.

Psychotherapy can become one of man's most notable services to man, and through man, to God. The Christian

Gospel is God's fullest manifestation of His love and concern for man—and Christianity is commissioned to that service, in every area and dimension of human life. There is, then, no justifiable basis for rivalry between the two as if they were *both* religions! On the contrary, there is every good reason for alliance between them in their respective spheres. As psychotherapists are willing to learn from the Christian evangel, many of them will discover that it is the power and wisdom of God for man's true health and salvation. And as Christians are willing to learn from the great and growing store of clinical truth in psychotherapy, they will find a fresh confirmation that God has many witnesses to His grace who do not know His Name—and yet these also He would bring into the community of His love.

The three alternatives before us are quite unequal. Before a religion masquerading as science, or a religion supported by poor science, thoughtful men are bound to recoil. But if a good science makes way for an honest alliance with high religion, and religion opens its eyes ungrudgingly to the growing light of good science, we would then have a notable alliance and collaboration, in which men of faith and fine intelligence might freely join in common devotion to God who made man's mind to praise Him, and in common service to mankind, in which we may show forth our love of God.

NOTES

CHAPTER ONE. *Allies and Rivals*

1. Cf. Report #7, *Hospital Committee of the Group for the Advancement of Psychiatry* (March, 1949), for the most conservative figure; cf. J. Wilder, "Facts and Figures on Psychotherapy," *Journal of Clinical Psychology*, VII (1945), for the highest estimate. M. Fishbein, "Mental Hygiene," *Hygeia* XXVII (1949) obviously defines neurosis in very broad terms. H. J. Eyesenk reports on the English statistics in *Dimensions of Personality* (1947).

2. Cf. J. T. McNeill, *A History of the Cure of Souls* (Harper, 1951), for a detailed and highly instructive account of the development of the patterns of Christian counseling and pastoral care. A great deal of the new wisdom of psychotherapy has its adumbration in the pastoral wisdom of good Christian priests and ministers.

3. Among the very few books of this sort, by far the best is David E. Roberts, *Psychotherapy and a Christian View of Man* (Scribner's, 1950); it is almost equally valuable for its competent summary description of psychotherapy and the steady clarity of its Christian view of man. For a Roman Catholic evaluation of psychotherapy, cf. James H. Van der Veldt and R. P. Odenwald, *Psychiatry and Catholicism* (McGraw-Hill, 1952). See also L. D. Weatherhead, *Psychology, Religion and Healing* (Abingdon-Cokesbury Press, 1951), and the symposium "Christian Faith and Psychotherapy" in *Religion in Life* (Autumn, 1952), by Weatherhead, Hiltner and Outler.

4. Among the historical surveys, the best I know are Freud's own *Early Papers* and his *On The History of the Psycho-Analytic Movement* (1914) (*Collected Papers*, I), Patrick Mullahy, *Oedipus Myth and Complex; A Review of Psychoanalytic Theory* (Hermitage Press, 1948), and Clara Thompson, *Psychoanalysis, Evolution and Development: A Review of Theory and Therapy* (Hermitage Press, 1950).

5. Cf. W. Wolff, *The Threshold of the Abnormal* (Medical Publications, 1952), pp. 293–308.

6. I agree, at least in part, with Dr. W. C. Menninger's distinction between the professional psychotherapist and the lay counselor. "Advisory counselling given by clergymen, teachers, lawyers, nurses, parents, and others to their constituency is not psychotherapy (in the strict sense). Psychotherapy, a formalized method to alleviate illness or maladjustment, requires an extensive (medical) training." "The Relationship of Clinical Psychology and Psychiatry," *The Bulletin of the Menninger Clinic*, XIV, 1 (1950), p. 1. This absolute disjunction between professional and lay therapy is, of course, much too sharp and reflects the pride of the doctors' guild that only they can cure. However, it is a prime element in ministerial wisdom to know the limits of one's competence in dealing with emotionally disturbed persons—and to have an adequate arrangement for referral. The Christian minister is interested in psychotherapy, therefore, not because he aims to practice without a license, but because he is in constant and intimate association with people whose crises and problems he can better understand with the help of the practical wisdom of psychotherapy. It is this wisdom, rather than medical or pseudo-medical knowledge, which is most useful to productive work with individuals.

7. Cf. the excellent discussion of the prerequisites for successful therapy in Frieda Fromm-Reichmann, *Principles of Intensive Psychotherapy* (University of Chicago Press, 1950), Pt. I, pp. 7–39, and also chap. III, "How Therapy Works," in Roberts, *op. cit.*, pp. 33–55.

8. Cf. Otto Fenichel, *The Psychoanalytic Theory of Neurosis* (Routledge & Kegan Paul, 1945), p. 31. See also Freud, *The Ego and the Id* (Hogarth Press, 1927), pp. 79, 83.

9. Cf. *Collected Papers*, II, p. 354. See also Fromm-Reichmann, *op. cit.*, p. 11.

10. Fromm-Reichmann, *op. cit.*, p. 12.

11. Matt. 20:25–28.

12. Many, though certainly not all, of the better-known cases of "faith healing" would fall under this general heading. Cf. Leslie Weatherhead, *op. cit.*, sections I–III, for a review of this problem. And cf. F. Alexander, *Psychosomatic Medicine* (Norton, 1950), for a standard analysis of the correlation between emotional disorder and bodily malfunction.

13. Cf. Karen Horney's phrase, "the tyranny of the shoulds," and her analysis of the defects of moralism in *Neurosis and Human Growth* (Norton, 1949), pp. 64 ff.

14. Cf. J. H. Hadfield, *Psychology and Mental Health* (Allen & Unwin, 1950), p. 321: "Propitiatory obsession is the outward and visible sign of an inward lack of grace. . . . It is easier to bare one's head than one's soul, to make the sign of the Cross than to bear one, to wash the hands than to cleanse the soul."

15. Cf. Roy S. Lee, *Freud and Christianity* (James Clarke, 1948), p. 55.

16. Cf. W. Wolff, *op. cit.*, p. 262.

17. Cf. Suttie's elaboration of Ferenczi's dictum that "it is the physician's love that heals the patient" in *The Origins of Love and Hate* (Kegan Paul, 1935), p. 75 et seq.

18. *The Heavenly City of the 18th Century Philosophers* (Yale University Press, 1932). See also Crane Brinton, *Ideas and Men* (Prentice-Hall, 1950), chap. 11.

19. Cf. C. Becker, *op. cit.*, pp. 102–3.

20. *Ibid.*, p. 50. See also Crane Brinton, *op. cit.*, p. 377.

21. *Op. cit.*, p. 369.

22. Cf. Becker, *op. cit.*, pp. 140 f., where he quotes Robespierre's invocation of posterity as to God and Priestley's rapt vision of a future age of mankind as "glorious and paradisiacal beyond what our imagination can now conceive."

23. *Ibid.*, p. 130.

24. The best known, perhaps: Sigmund Freud, *The Future of an Illusion* (Hogarth Press, 1928); Erich Fromm, *Man for Himself* (Rinehart, 1947), *Religion and Psychoanalysis* (Yale Uni-

versity Press, 1950); J. C. Flugel, *Man, Morals and Society* (Duckworth, 1945), chap. XVII; Marjorie Brierley, *Trends in Psychoanalysis* (Hogarth Press, 1951); Franz Alexander, *An Age of Unreason* (Lippincott, 1951), chaps. IX–XI.

25. Cf. C. S. Sherrington's exposition of the concept of nature in Jean Fernel and his colleagues in *Man on His Nature* (Macmillan, 1941), p. 62 *et seq.* See also R. G. Collingwood, *The Idea of Nature* (Oxford, 1945), pp. 93–116.

26. Cf. H. Hoffding, *A History of Modern Philosophy* (Macmillan, 1900), II, p. 499 *et seq.* See also W. K. Wright, *A History of Modern Philosophy* (Macmillan, 1941), pp. 445 ff.

27. Cf. Freud, *Collected Papers*, IV, p. 18; see also V, pp. 92 f., 244 f., 234 f.; *The Future of an Illusion*, p. 55.

28. Cf. the last sentence of *The Future of an Illusion:* "No, science is no illusion. But it would be an illusion to suppose we could get anywhere else what it cannot give us" (p. 98). See also p. 55.

29. *Religion in Life, op. cit.*, p. 500. Note that Hiltner believes that the development of modern psychotherapy has its roots in the Christian tradition! There is a sense in which all modern secular humanitarianism does. But the explicit source *ideas* of modern psychotherapy's world view are either non- or anti-Christian.

30. Cf. Patrick Mullahy in *The Contribution of Harry Stack Sullivan* (Hermitage, 1952), pp. 15–18.

31. Eph. 4:13–15.

CHAPTER TWO. *The Human Self and Its Freedom*

1. Cf. "On the History of the Psycho-Analytic Movement," *Collected Papers*, I, pp. 314–15.

2. For a brief biographical sketch, see *Dictionary of American Biography*, 15, pp. 282–83. Freud generously acknowledged his help: "His high moral character and unflenching love of truth was of great service to psychoanalysis and protected it against the denunciations which might otherwise have early overwhelmed it." *Collected Papers*, I, p. 315.

3. All these papers are included in Putnam's posthumous *Ad-*

dresses on Psychoanalysis (International Psychoanalytic Press, 1921).

4. Freud, *Collected Papers*, I, p. 315; cf. II, p. 399.

5. *Op. cit.*, p. iv.

6. *Ibid.*, p. 463.

7. Pp. 86 ff. On p. 448, Putnam tells of a remark made by Freud at their first meeting at Worcester. He (Putnam) had been arguing that Freud's biologism seemed to rule out moral evaluation of human acts and implied "automatic and necessary reactions to specific and determinable causes. To this Freud replied, with impressive earnestness, that it was not moral estimates that were needed for solving the problems of human life and motives but more *knowledge*." This outlook, Putnam believed, had come to typify the whole movement—"until it came to stand in my mind as a testimony, alike to the strength and to the weakness, of the great movement to which Freud has dedicated his life!"

8. *The Spirit of Medieval Philosophy* (Scribner's, 1936), p. 195.

9. Cf. Athenagoras, *The Resurrection of the Dead*, XV.

10. "Persona est naturae rationalis individua substantia." *De Persona et Duabis Naturis*, III, in Migne, *Patrologia Latina*, 75, p. 1343.

11. Cf. Gilson, *op. cit.*, p. 203. See also Christopher Devlin, *The Psychology of Duns Scotus* (Black Friars, 1950), pp. 4–5.

12. Cf. William Temple, *Nature, Man and God* (Macmillan, 1934), pp. 51–81. See also E. Gilson, *The Unity of Philosophical Experience* (Scribner's, 1937), Pts. Two and Three.

13. Cf. *The Critique of Pure Reason*, "Deduction of the Pure Concepts of Understanding" (Smith's translation), pp. 141–69.

14. Cf. Gardner Murphy, *Personality* (Harper, 1947), Pt. Four. And see also D. C. McClelland, *Personality* (Sloane, 1951), pp. 3–18.

15. "A few [sic!] psychologists are still unconsciously so close to their possessive mother, philosophy, and to their dogmatic grandfather, theology, that they are compelled to assert their autonomy and self-sufficiency in the most radical possible manner, by adopting the extreme position of nineteenth-century mechanism." Clyde K. Kluckhohn and Henry A. Murray (eds.),

Personality in Nature, Society and Culture (Knopf, 1948), p. 14.

16. Cf., e.g., Kluckhohn and Murray, *op. cit.*, pp. 8–9. Personality, they say, *"must be located in nature, within some field where there is a togetherness of all these processes or of representations of all these processes. . . .* Thus we can state that personality is the *organization of all the integrative (regnant) processes in the brain."* Only this, and nothing more?

17. P. Mullahy, in *The Contributions of Harry Stack Sullivan,* p. 16. See also William James, *Psychology, Briefer Course* (1892), p. 203.

18. Cf. Austin Farrer, *Finite and Infinite* (Dacre Press, 1943), pp. vi–vii, and chaps. X–XIX. This is, in my judgment, the most profound and truly productive analysis of the idea of human will and selfhood since Kant—and far more Christian than Kant. Has its general neglect by the professional metaphysicians been due to the great difficulties of its style—or to its highly explicit theistic "bias"?

19. Cf. Reinhold Niebuhr, *The Nature and Destiny of Man* (Scribner's, 1941), Vol. I, chap. VI, for a summary exposition of the Christian concept of the self.

20. Kluckhohn and Murray, *op. cit.*, p. 9.

21. H. S. Sullivan, *Conceptions of Modern Psychiatry* (Wm. A. White Psychiatric Foundation, 1947), pp. 19–21.

22. Otto Fenichel, *The Psychoanalytic Theory of Neurosis,* p. 16.

23. Cf. L. Hinsie, *The Person in the Body* (Norton, 1945), pp. 205–6.

24. *Op. cit.*, p. 43.

25. *Op. cit.*, p. 43.

26. Cf. P. Mullahy, *Oedipus, Myth and Complex,* pp. 292 ff.

27. *Op. cit.*, p. 10. Cf. Mead, *Mind, Self and Society* (University of Chicago Press, 1934).

28. The same general viewpoint is to be seen in a large group of psychotherapists (e.g., Thompson, Mullahy, Fromm-Reichmann, Fromm, *et al.*). Cf. Clara Thompson, *Psychoanalysis, Evolution and Development,* pp. 292 ff., for a survey; cf. Mullahy, *op. cit.*, for a refinement and extension of the Sullivanesque approach.

29. Cf. W. Wolff, *Threshold of the Abnormal,* pp. 192–93.

30. Sir Charles Sherrington, *Man on His Nature* (Macmillan, 1941), pp. 356–57. Cf. *ibid.*, pp. 389, 318–19.
31. *Collected Papers*, IV, p. 119. Cf. *New Introductory Lectures on Psychoanalysis* (Norton, 1933), pp. 103 ff.
32. I Cor. 13:12.
33. Karl Jaspers, *Perennial Scope of Philosophy* (Routledge & Kegan Paul, 1950), pp. 66–67. Cf. S. Kierkegaard, *Sickness unto Death* (Princeton University Press, 1941), pp. 27 f.
34. Cf. Karl Jaspers, *Way to Wisdom* (Victor Gollancz, 1951), p. 117. See also Jaspers' retort to Nietzsche: "Only with his eyes to God does man grow instead of seeping away undammed into the meaninglessness of life's mere happenings."
35. Cf. P. Mullahy, "Will, Choice and Ends," *Psychiatry*, XII, 4, p. 382: "There is no *special* mystery about man or about mind, but man and mind are harder to understand and harder to explain." So they are, indeed!
36. Cf. H. J. Paton, *The Categorical Imperative* (Hutchinson's University Library, 1946), pp. 227–28, where he shows that Kant's full thesis in his first two *Critiques* is (a) the delimitation of positive knowledge and (b) the reassertion of the objective reality and plenary fullness of being—itself.
37. "Determinism, 'Freedom' and Psychotherapy," *Psychiatry*, IX (August, 1946), pp. 251–62.
38. "Will, Choice and Ends," *Psychiatry*, XII (November, 1949), pp. 382–86.
39. *Op. cit.*, pp. 383, 384.
40. I. Kant, *Critique of Practical Reason* (Beck translation), p. 152.
41. Farrer, *op. cit.*, p. 115.
42. *Ibid.*, p. 116. Cf. the entirety of Farrer's extended and intricate argument, in chaps. X and XI. One can hardly profess to have a fully considered judgment on the nature of will until he has taken Farrer into full account. And I would think that the psychotherapists might take the trouble to read him, since he goes as far as a Christian can to make common cause with naturalism.
43. Cf. *ibid.*, p. 108: "We have no awareness of the time-lag between any object that is to our apprehension immediate, and our apprehension of it. Everything has happened by the time we see it happening; but we are not aware of this."

CHAPTER THREE. *The Human Quandary*

1. *Conceptions of Modern Psychiatry*, p. 27.
2. "Song of Myself," Canto 32, in *Leaves of Grass* (Doubleday, 1940), p. 68. Used by permission of the publisher.
3. Sullivan, *op. cit.*, p. 48.
4. The fact of "the unconscious mind" is, of course, an inference since it is, by definition, nonperceptible. But it is a very weighty inference, once one considers seriously the phenomena of free-association and dream work. It is hard to avoid the general conclusion that the dynamic springs of human action lie far below the levels of conscious and rational direction and control and that there is an intrapsychic tension between the "unconscious drives" and our consciously approved ends and means.
5. Cf. the description of this phase in C. Berg, *Psychotherapy: Practice and Theory* (Norton, 1948), pp. 427 f.
6. *An Outline of Psychoanalysis* (Norton, 1949), p. 29.
7. Freud, *op. cit.*, pp. 29–30.
8. Freud, *The Ego and the Id* (Hogarth Press, 1927), p. 79.
9. Freud, *An Outline of Psychoanalysis*, p. 17.
10. Freud's mature instinct theory included the idea of a *Thanatos* instinct which complements the functions of *Eros*. This has been a point of controversy and many devout Freudians have declined to follow him in this matter; cf. C. Thompson, *Psychoanalysis*, pp. 50–55 *et seq.* But it seems to me that there is as good *logic* in Freud's case for *Thanatos* as well as *Eros*. I do not presume to pass a judgment on the clinical evidence.
11. *Collected Papers*, V, p. 283; but see the whole letter as most revealing of Freud as a moralist.
12. Cf. Freud's very significant—penultimate—paper, "Analysis Terminable & Interminable" (1937), *Collected Papers*, V, pp. 316 ff.
13. Cf. the essay "On Transcience" written in November, 1915, as a reflection on the inevitable loss of cherished values and the destruction wrought by the war which, as he foresaw even then, was wrecking the foundations of European civilization. This is the most poignant note in all Freud's writings. *Collected Papers*, V, p. 287; and chap. XXX.

14. *Collected Papers*, V, p. 331.

15. Cf. his A *Study of Organ-Inferiority and Its Psychical Compensation* (Nervous and Mental Disease Monograph Series, No. 24. New York, 1917).

16. For a brief, appreciative summary of Adler's contributions, cf. Clara Thompson, *Psychoanalysis*, pp. 153-61. For a caustic criticism, cf. Freud's own "History of the Psychoanalytic Movement," in *Collected Papers*, I, pp. 339-47.

17. *Collected Papers on Analytical Psychology* (Balliere, Tindall & Cox, 1920), Preface pp. xiii-xiv.

18. *The Theory of Psychoanalysis* (Nervous and Mental Disease Monograph Series, No. 19. New York, 1915).

19. Cf. Mullahy, *op. cit.*, pp. 139 f.

20. Cf. *The Psychology of the Unconscious* (Moffat, Yard & Co., 1931). See also *The Integration of the Personality* (Farrar & Rinehart, 1939), pp. 13-29.

21. P. 264. Cf. also *Psychology & Religion* (Yale University Press, 1938), p. 76; see the whole essay as an example of Jung's conception of religion. But before any Christian rejoices at the prospect of Jung's support in the alliance between psychotherapy and Christianity, he should examine with care the Jungian world view and see the radical cleavage between such an avowed Gnosticism and any stable version of the Judeo-Christian theism.

22. Cf. *Psychological Types* (Harcourt, Brace, 1933).

23. One might comment in passing on the speculative character of many of these inferences about the intrauterine state. The wildest flights of fancy on this topic yet attempted may be found in Ron Hubbard's *Dianetics* (Hermitage House, 1950), where we have verbatim recollections of conversations heard by fetuses long before any auditory end organs were developed! For the soberest and most substantial account of present empirical knowledge on the subject, see George W. Corner's Terry Lectures for 1944, *Ourselves Unborn* (Yale University Press, 1944).

24. Cf. Clara Thompson, pp. 174-85. Our interest here is not in Rank's contributions to therapy but in his emphasis upon will and freedom as the pivot of the human quandary.

25. Cf. Thompson, *op. cit.*, chap. 9.

26. Cf. F. Alexander, *Fundamentals of Psychoanalysis* (Norton, 1948), pp. 276 ff. "The Chicago Psychoanalytic Institute's experiments with therapy have resurveyed the therapeutic process and re-emphasized the significance of emotional experiences during treatment, both in the transference and outside of the therapeutic situation, as the main therapeutic factor. Modern psychoanalytic therapy relies mainly on the handling of the transference." For a criticism and correction of Freud's instinctual theory, see pp. 61–75.

27. *Op. cit.*, p. 99.

28. *Op cit.*, chap. V, "The Function of the Ego and Its Failures."

29. Cf. *Our Age of Unreason* (Lippincott, 1951), p. 316:
"International cooperation based on conscience that does not know national boundaries.
"Social activity based on a mature creative power instead of adolescent competitiveness arising from insecurity.
"The development of new standards in which the creative use of the mind, contributing to knowledge, art, or the amenities of everyday life, stands high.
"The recognition of the fact that the development of the social sciences is at present more urgent than farther technical advance."

30. Jules H. Masserman, *Principles of Dynamic Psychiatry* (W. B. Saunders, 1946), p. 102. The three other basic principles are as follows:
"2. *Principle of Experimental Interpretation and Adaptation.* Behavior is contingent upon, and adaptive to, the organism's *interpretations* of its total milieu, as based upon its capacities and previous experiences.
"3. *Principle of Deviation and Substitution.* Behavior patterns become deviated and fragmented under stress, and when further frustrated, tend toward substitutive satisfactions.
"4. *Principle of Conflict.* When in a given milieu two or more motivations come into conflict in the sense that their accustomed consummatory patterns become incompatible kinetic tension (anxiety) mounts and behavior becomes hesitant, vacillating, erratic, and poorly adaptive (neurotic) or excessively substitutive, symbolic and regressive (psychotic)."

31. Here we might note, only in passing, the baldest and most

frankly amoral and subpersonal of all contemporary psychotherapeutic views of the human quandary: Andrew Salter's
Conditioned Reflex Therapy (Creative Age, 1949). This is
both a bitter attack upon Freudianism and also a passionate
elaboration of Pavlovian psychology. Its triumphant claim is
that "only science, absolute science" can save us. Its "single
precept: *The solution of all problems of the self comes from
the unbraking of the individual's behavior with other people*"
(p. 317); but see the whole of the chapter, "Only Science,
Absolute Science" (pp. 315 f.). Even if we waive the question
as to what sort of "science" this stuff is, it is difficult to see *any*
fruitful points of connection between such doctrinaire ma-
terialism and the Christian outlook.

32. H. S. Sullivan, *op. cit.*, pp. 4–5.

33. *Man for Himself*, p. 41. Cf. the entire section, pp. 38–50.

34. *Ibid.*, p. 42.

35. *Ibid.*, pp. 44–45. Cf. Becker, *The Heavenly City of the 18th
Century Philosophers*, pp. 14–15, 74, for parallels to this thesis
in Enlightenment thought.

36. H. R. Mackintosh, *The Christian Experience of Forgiveness*
(Harper, 1927), p. 61; see the whole of chap. III for a notable
analysis of the Christian ideas of sin and guilt.

37. Some of the standard surveys are: F. R. Tennant, *The Sources
of the Doctrine of the Fall and Original Sin* (Macmillan,
1903); N. P. Williams, *Ideas of the Fall and of Original Sin*
(Longmans, 1927); Reinhold Niebuhr, *The Nature and Destiny of Man*.

38. Cave, *The Christian Estimate of Man* (Duckworth, 1944),
p. 219.

39. Reinhold Niebuhr, *op. cit.*, I, pp. 182–86. This particular section of this book (chaps. 7 and 8) contains the most significant
analysis of the dynamism and morphology of sin in contemporary Christian theology. Niebuhr is an outstanding example
of the modern theologian, himself deeply influenced by psychotherapy, who seeks to restate the basic Christian doctrine
of man in the light of the Gospel and new knowledge. The
historical section of the book has many faults but the constructive section in the chapters cited above is likely to remain
as a *classic* statement of the Christian message in this area.

40. *Psychoanalysis and Religion*, pp. 34–53.
41. Cf. the profound and poignant analysis of the Christian analysis of man's plight in Robert L. Calhoun, *What Is Man?* (Association Press, 1939), pp. 68–73.
42. Cf. an interesting and practical reminder of this in Don P. Morris, "Flexibility & Experimentation in Psychotherapy," *Diseases of the Nervous System* (University of Texas Medical School, March, 1950), pp. 83–85.

CHAPTER FOUR. *The Human Possibility*

1. "I described this as the *psychological* blow to men's narcissism, and compared it with the *biological* blow delivered by the theory of descent and the earlier *cosmological* blow aimed at it by the discovery of Copernicus." *Collected Papers*, V, p. 173.
2. *Collected Papers*, V, pp. 81–82.
3. *The Future of an Illusion*, pp. 52 ff.
4. Cf. the chapter on "A Philosophy of Life" in the *New Introductory Lectures on Psychoanalysis*, pp. 216–49.
5. Cf. Mullahy, *Oedipus*, pp. 123 f.
6. Cf. Pt. VII, sec. iv.
7. *Psychoanalysis*, p. 168. See also Jung, *Two Essays on Analytical Psychology* (Dodd, Mead & Co., 1928), pp. 186 f.
8. Cf. Hans Schaer, *Religion and the Cure of Souls in Jung's Psychology* (Pantheon, 1950), pp. 94–95.
9. Cf. the estimate of Sullivan and a tribute to his sacrificial devotion to the cause of mental health in Brock Chisholm, "New Vistas of Responsibility," *Psychiatry* (May, 1949), pp. 191–95.
10. "Progressively, in the course of identifying all the more important parataxically surviving, unresolved situations of the patient's past, and their consequent dissolutions, there goes an *expanding of the self* to such final effect that the patient as known to himself is much the same person as the patient behaving with others. This is *psychiatric* cure. There may remain a need for a great deal of experience and education before the psychiatric cure is a *social* cure, implying a more abundant life in the community." *Op. cit.*, p. 117.
11. *Ibid.*, p. 26.

12. For summary estimates, cf. P. Mullahy. *Oedipus*, chap. 8; and C. Thompson, *Psychoanalysis*, pp. 197–203.

13. *Neurosis and Human Growth*, pp. 15–16.

14. *Op. cit.*, p. 363.

15. *Ibid.*, p. 364.

16. This type corresponds to Horney's description of neurotic appeasement in what she calls "the compliant type." Cf. *Our Inner Conflicts* (Norton, 1945), p. 49 *et seq.*

17. *Man for Himself*, pp. 84–88.

18. *Ibid.*, p. 114.

19. *Ibid.*, p. 25.

20. *Ibid.*, p. 34.

21. *Ibid.*, p. 35.

22. *Ibid.*, p. 53.

23. *Ibid.*, p. 49.

24. *Escape from Freedom* (Rinehart, 1941), pp. 144 ff. This is probably not the place to examine the historical validity of this and other sweeping generalizations which Dr. Fromm so readily makes. It is enough to note that a very good psychiatrist may nevertheless be something less than adequate as a historian of ideas.

25. Hogarth Press, 1951, pp. 16, 159 f.

26. *Man, Morals and Society*, p. 275.

27. Cf. *Escape from Freedom*, pp. 155–56.

28. Fromm, *Man for Himself*, p. 91.

29. Cf. my essay, "For Us Men and Our Salvation," *Religion in Life* (Spring, 1951), pp. 163–79, for a summary treatment on the mode and meaning of Christian salvation. For an ampler exploration, see H. R. Mackintosh, *The Christian Experience of Forgiveness*, or Leonard Hodgson, *The Doctrine of the Atonement* (Nisbet, 1951).

30. Cf. Richard Niebuhr, *Christ and Culture* (Harper, 1951), especially chap. 6.

31. Gal. 5:22–23a.

32. I Cor. 2:9.

33. I John 3:2.

34. Cf. Reinhold Niebuhr, *The Nature and Destiny of Man*, II, *pp.* 213 ff.; see the whole volume as an important example of

the antiperfectionist trend in contemporary Christian theology.

35. C. Lamont, *The Illusion of Immortality* (Philosophical Library, 1950), p. 278.
36. *Ibid.*, p. 288.
37. Cf. Fromm, *Man for Himself*, pp. 42–44.
38. Cf. A. E. Taylor, *The Christian Hope of Immortality* (Centenary Press, 1938); John Baillie, *And the Life Everlasting* (Scribner's, 1933); R. J. Campbell, *The Life of the World to Come* (Longmans, 1948) as quite various analyses of the common Christian hope of man's destiny.
39. Col. 2:16–18, 3:12–15.
40. 2 Cor. 4:1–5:6.
41. Robert L. Calhoun, *What Is Man?*, p. 73.

CHAPTER FIVE. *The Ordering of Life*

1. J. C. Flugel, *Man, Morals and Society*, p. 247.
2. F. Rabelais, *Gargantua and Pantagruel*, I, lvii.
3. *The Future of an Illusion*, p. 76.
4. *Ibid.*, p. 84. He adds, "Should it prove unsatisfactory, I am ready to give up the reform." Freud lived to see nonreligious education come to be the rule rather than the exception in Western civilization. But the experiment has not been controlled and its results have not proved "satisfactory" to either proponents or opponents of secularism.
5. *Op. cit.*, Chaps. II, III.
6. *Ibid.*, p. 240.
7. According to Flugel, valid moral growth shows progress in the following respects: from autism to realism; from moral inhibitions to spontaneous goodness; from aggression to tolerance and love; from fear to security; from heteronomy to autonomy; from orectic judgments to cognitive judgments. For a descriptive analysis of each of these "progressions," see chap. XVI.
8. *Ibid.*, p. 260.
9. Pp. 272–75. Flugel is aware of the influence in his own ethical theory and the evolutionary morality of Herbert Spencer. Cf. pp. 257–58.
10. *Neurosis and Human Growth*, pp. 347–77.
11. *Ibid.*, p. 378.

12. *Psychoanalysis and Religion* (Yale University Press, 1950), p. 87.
13. *Idem.*
14. Pp. 118–19.
15. *Conceptions of Modern Psychiatry*, p. 87.
16. Macmillan, 1951.
17. Neuchâtel, 1947.
18. *Op. cit.*, p. 47. Cf. the whole of chap. II.
19. *Ibid.*, p. 73. In italics in the original.
20. *Ibid.*, pp. 195–202.
21. *Ibid.*, pp. 219–20.
22. *Op. cit.*, p. 40.
23. *Op. cit.*, pp. 211–39.
24. *Ibid.*, p. 221.
25. *Idem.*
26. *The Psychoanalytic Theory of Neurosis*, p. 589.
27. One of the most impressive accounts of what is achieved in effective therapy and how the changes are experienced is Lucy Freeman, *Fight against Fears* (Crown Publishers, 1951). Cf. especially chaps. XX–XXII. "Some friends remarked, 'You're no different today from the way you were five years ago, except you're a little calmer.' But that marks quite a difference, I thought. A little calm, where before no calm existed, denotes much control." (P. 293.) See the rest of this section for a report on the emergence of new feelings of kindliness, understanding and love.
28. Cf. *Collected Papers*, IV, p. 316.
29. Cf. Brock Chisholm, "New Vistas of Responsibility," *Psychiatry* (May, 1949), pp. 191–95.
30. Cf. *A Common Faith* (Yale University Press, 1934).
31. *The Source of Human Good* (University of Chicago Press, 1946), pp. 6–7. Cf. also chaps. I, III, IX, X, for an attempt to assimilate the Christian wisdom into naturalistic categories. As so often happens, he can get a good many Christian ideas into his system—but not the Christian God! (Pp. 7, 49–50, 264–68, 305–9.) The result is not altogether stable.
32. *Ibid.*, pp. 77–80.
33. *Op. cit.*, p. 15.
34. *Man for Himself*, p. 45.

35. *Op. cit.*, p. 280.

36. Cf. Paul Ramsey, *Basic Christian Ethics* (Scribner's, 1950), chap. II.

37. T. W. Manson, *The Teaching of Jesus* (Cambridge, 1932), p. 312.

38. Major, Manson and Wright, *The Mission and Message of Jesus* (Dutton, 1938), pp. 321 ff.

39. B. Harvie Branscomb, *The Teachings of Jesus* (Cokesbury Press, 1931), pp. 293 ff.

40. T. W. Manson, *op. cit.*, p. 299.

41. Mark 8:34–36. Cf. Matt. 16:24–28; Luke 9:23–24.

42. Luke 14:33.

43. I Cor. 6:19b–20; 7:23. Cf. Ramsey, *op. cit.*, chap. III; and see also Major, Manson and Wright, *op. cit.*, pp. iii f., 422 ff.

44. Matt. 6:33

45. Cf. M.C. D'Arcy, *The Mind and Heart of Love* (Holt, 1947), pp. 11–16, and chaps. VI, X and XIV. This is a most significant synthesis of Christian ideas of love, much more fully balanced than Nygren's famous *Eros and Agape*.

46. I John 4:10–11.

47. P. Ramsey, *op. cit.*, p. 209.

48. There is the authentic note of "permanent ethical revolution" in the Magnificat (Luke 1:46–53) which is sometimes missed by the upper middle class congregations who intone it with more solemnity than urgency.

49. Cf. Mark 11:25, Matt. 6:14 f; see also Manson, *op. cit.*, p. 311.

50. Rom. 5:20.

51. Cf. H. Richard Niebuhr, *The Meaning of Revelation* (Macmillan, 1941), chap. I, for a highly significant exposition of this thesis.

52. Col. 1:13–14.

CHAPTER SIX. *The Terms of the Alliance*

1. Freud, *The Future of an Illusion*, p. 98.

2. "Nothing in Newtonian (or recent) science need have caused a breakdown of religious faith. But the modern mind has supposed that it must. Nothing in it (science) excludes belief in a cosmic purpose. But the modern mind has supposed that it

does. Nothing in it has any tendency to prove that the world is not a moral order. Yet the world has drawn from it that conclusion. All these fancied implications of science are logical muddles." W. T. Stace, *Religion and the Modern Mind* (Lippincott, 1952), p. 126. Cf. Whitehead, *Science and the Modern World* (Macmillan, 1931), chaps. XI–XII; and Tillich, *Systematic Theology* (University of Chicago Press, 1950), I, pp. 230–33; *cf.* also pp. 18 ff.

3. F. W. Nietzsche, *Thus Spake Zarathustra*, V, 2.
4. Cf. Stace, *op. cit.*, p. 127. See also E. Brunner, *Christianity and Civilization* (Nisbet, 1948), I, chaps. VI–VII.
5. Cf. K. Jaspers, *Way to Wisdom*, pp. 86–87.
6. K. Jaspers, *The Perennial Scope of Philosophy* (Routledge & Kegan Paul, 1950), pp. 38–42. See also Stace, *Religion and the Modern Mind*, p. 143. There is a climactic passage in Flugel which is almost poignant in its claim that mature men must rise above the superstitions of transcendental religion:

"And here the final ineluctable renunciation must be made. Men must abandon the last shred of that longed-for but illusory 'omnipotence' to which, even after the relinquishing of magic, they sought to cling through their relation with a divine ruler of the universe. Prayer and sacrifice, the hope for miracles, are, as usually understood, useless, if our gods themselves are only human and enjoy no jurisdiction beyond the range of human power. The vaster universe around us appears to be indifferent to human hopes and sufferings, and we must, it seems, resign ourselves to accept the teaching of Omar Khayyam:

> And that inverted Bowl we call The Sky,
> Whereunder crawling coop't we live and die,
> Lift not thy hands to It for help—for It
> Rolls impotently on as Thou or I.

"A terrible lesson, which cannot perhaps be learnt without incurring a bitter sense of loss and loneliness. Men are in fact thrown back upon themselves and must rely on their own efforts to improve their lot. But this very sense of loneliness and isolation may well serve to bring them closer together than would otherwise be possible; and they have the consolation of knowing that in the human heart and brain they possess instruments which, faulty though they be, have brought them far along the path of evolution, and, if wisely used, may bring them almost infinitely farther. We have ample proof that courage and intelligence, though they never perform miracles, will yet achieve what a generation or two earlier would have been considered miracles. Within his sphere of influence (which is so rapidly expanding) man himself is far from being impotent and, as Freud reminds us in the last passage of his earlier book on religion, science at least has no appearance of being an 'illusion.' And if this view should still seem intolerably bleak, we can, as was indicated at the end of the last chapter, perhaps derive some comfort from the thought that man, with all his powers and possibilities (as yet so largely unexploited), is himself a product of evolution. If there is a purpose in evolution, we have no means of understanding it except in and through the mind of man. There is no guidance as to the nature of this purpose and our place in it save such as we ourselves provide through the free use of human faculty." *Op. cit.*, pp. 280–81.

7. Stace is very emphatic in his charge: "There is no doubt that naturalism, with its corollary of the futility of human life, has brought despair into the world. It is the root-cause of the modern spiritual malaise. . . . The spiritual darkness of the modern mind has its source in the scientific view of the world." (p. 208.) Cf. Jaspers, Sartre and Kierkegaard.

8. F. R. Tennant, *Philosophical Theology* (Cambridge University Press, 1928–1930), II p. 121 *et seq.* Tennant's empirical rejection of naturalism is significant for he certainly tried to go with the scientists and empirical philosophers as far as he could in understanding and interpreting the data of existence.

9. Cf. K. Jaspers, *The Perennial Scope of Philosophy*, p. 34. See also his *Way to Wisdom*, pp. 43 ff. for a shrewd analysis of the incompleteness of naturalism.

10. William Temple, *Nature, Man and God*, p. 265. See this whole section for a cogent statement of the rationale for theism. See also R. L. Calhoun, *God and the Common Life*, chaps. III and IV, and A. E. Taylor, *The Faith of a Moralist* (Macmillan, 1937), I, 6.

11. One should note, in this connection, the criticisms which have

been made of VanderVeldt and Odenwald, *Psychiatry and Catholicism*—and, especially, from their fellow Catholics. And cf., as a significant recent Roman contribution to our discussion, Joseph Nuttin, *Psychoanalysis and Personality* (Sheed and Ward, 1953).

INDEX

283